Disability, Augmentative Communication, and the American Dream

Disability, Augmentative Communication, and the American Dream

A Qualitative Inquiry

Ronald J. Berger, Jon A. Feucht, and Jennifer Flad

LEXINGTON BOOKS
Lanham • Boulder • New York • Toronto • Plymouth, UK

KH

Published by Lexington Books
A wholly owned subsidiary of Rowman & Littlefield
4501 Forbes Boulevard, Suite 200, Lanham, Maryland 20706
www.rowman.com

10 Thornbury Road, Plymouth PL6 7PP, United Kingdom

British Library Cataloguing in Publication Information Available

Library of Congress Cataloging-in-Publication Data Available
ISBN 978-0-7391-8894-1 (cloth : alk. paper)—ISBN 978-0-7391-8895-8 (electronic)
ISBN 978-1-4985-2087-4 (pbk : alk. paper)

∞™ The paper used in this publication meets the minimum requirements of American National Standard for Information Sciences Permanence of Paper for Printed Library Materials, ANSI/NISO Z39.48-1992.

Printed in the United States of America

11/17/16

As this boy sits weeks away from his piece of history . . .
Thinking about everything he has been through
But knowing he's still in the prologue
Of his amazing story

His heart hungers to meet the person he is
Why do so many people love him?
What makes people to live and breathe
On every word that he says

—Jon Feucht, "The Late of the Early"

The communication device under my fingers
Is my piano
My hands float over the keys
Making beautiful sounds like they do
Even though I can't sing like Joel, John and others
My words are my art.
I can romance women; I can make people laugh,
And move young people like Lennon did . . .
Will I become a legend of my field?
Will I leave a legacy?

—Jon Feucht, "Keyboard Man"

Contents

Preface

Disability, Augmentative Communication, and the American Dream is a collaborative effort to tell the life story of Jon Feucht, a man who was born with a form of cerebral palsy that left him impaired in his lower and upper body and unable to speak without use of an assistive communication device. It is a story about finding one's voice, about defying low expectations, about fulfilling one's dreams, and about making a difference in the world. Jon earned his master's degree in special education at the University of Wisconsin-Whitewater and is currently working on a doctorate in educational leadership and policy at East Tennessee State University. He is also the founding director of Authentic Voices of America (AVA), an innovative summer camp for adolescents and young adults learning to use augmentative communication to speak.

The sociologist C. Wright Mills (1959) famously called for a "sociological imagination" that grapples with the intersection of biography and history in society and the ways in which personal troubles are related to public issues. We aim to heed this call by situating Jon's life in broader social context, by understanding disability not just as an individual experience but as a social phenomenon. In the tradition of disability studies, we also aim to illuminate an experience of disability that avoids reading it as tragic or pitiable.

We compiled the "data" for our study through a qualitative mixed methods approach that includes Jon's written narrative, interviews by Ron and Jennifer with Jon and significant others, and participant observation by Ron in various social milieus. Chapter 1 introduces our study, providing the conceptual, medical, technological, and methodological background that is relevant to our inquiry. Chapters 2–4, the life history portion of the book, tell the story of Jon's life from childhood through his college years, involvement in

AVA, and marriage. Chapters 5–6, the participant observation portion of the book, offer ethnographic accounts of social milieus that provide additional windows into the world of disability and augmentative-alternative communication. Lastly, chapter 7 concludes the book with an analytical summary of Jon's life in social context, including Jon's valuation of the American dream and our interest in the moral vision of multiculturalism as a vital feature of inclusion in the democratic project of human societies.

Disability, Augmentative Communication, and the American Dream is intended as an analytical and empirical contribution to both disability studies and qualitative sociology, to be read by social science scholars and students taking courses in disability studies and qualitative research, as well as by professionals working in the fields of special education and speech pathology. Written in an accessible style, the book will also be of interest to lay readers who want to learn more about disability issues and the disability experience.

We would like to thank Michael Ames, Jeremy Brunson, Norman Denzin, and Doug Hartmann for their helpful suggestions and endorsement of our work that has come to fruition in this book. We are appreciative, too, of the entire Feucht family, as well as David Travis and Connie Wiersma, for contributing their insights and experiences. We also thank Lynn and Maria Braun for their help with selecting the AVA photos, and Jana Hodges-Kluck and the staff of Lexington Books for their support of this book.

Introduction

Chapter One

Disability and the Individual in Society

Disability, Augmentative Communication, and the American Dream is a collaborative effort to illuminate the phenomenon of disability by telling the life story of Jon Feucht, a man who was born with a form of cerebral palsy (CP)—a condition caused by trauma to the brain before, during, or shortly after birth—that left him reliant on a wheelchair for mobility, with limited use of his arms and an inability to speak without an assistive communication device. Simultaneously, the book is an exemplar of what C. Wright Mills (1959) called the "sociological imagination," a sociology that grapples with the intersection of biography and history in society and the ways in which personal troubles are related to public issues. By linking personal stories to collective narratives, this sensitizing framework aims to reveal the world of ordinary people's lived experience and show how society "speaks itself" through the lives of individuals. As such, it strives for a sociology that makes the individual a fundamental reference point for analyzing empirical reality without placing the individual outside of his or her social context (Alexander 1988; Berger 2008a; Clandinin 2013; Rosenwald and Ochberg 1992).

Too often, we believe, social science scholars invoke Mills without exploring the full ramifications of his key insights regarding the relationship between the individual and society (Berger 2008a).[1] In this book we aim to heed Mills's call through a sociological study of Jon's life and the world of augmentative communication, and by understanding disability not just as an individual experience but as a social phenomenon. Although we aim for analytical understanding, we also want to tell a story that creates empathy, builds social bonds, and illuminates an experience of disability that resists reading it as tragic or pitiable and makes it more difficult to stigmatize or marginalize others (Berger and Quinney 2005; Clandinin 2013; Couser 2013;

1

Taylor 2001). At the same time, we don't wish to characterize Jon's story as a matter of "overcoming" his disability, when, in fact, his physical condition *is* his way of being *embodied* in the world (Baker 2011; Fries 1997; Linton 1998). Neither do we want to characterize Jon as some sort of "supercrip" whose inspirational story of courage, dedication, and hard work proves that it is possible to defy the odds and accomplish the impossible (Berger 2008b). It is not that we are opposed to readers finding Jon's story inspirational; indeed, we hope they will. It is simply that we do not want people to think that Jon or anyone else is a "self-made man" who can make it on their own without the help of family and other social supports, as well as the contemporary disability rights movement, without which Jon's story would arguably be impossible. Rather, we wonder, along with John Hockenberry, why people with disabilities are not a "source of reassurance . . . that although life is unpredictable and circumstances may be unfavorable, versatility and adaptation are possible" (quoted in Fleischer and Zames 2001:205). And in telling the story of someone who has "risen to the occasion" and refused to give in to despair, we hope to encourage others to "take comfort that even the worst life has to offer," as Daniel Taylor believes, "can be given shape, can be expressed—enacted—and therefore contemplated and reconciled" (2001:75).

In this chapter, we provide the conceptual background for understanding disability as a social phenomenon. We also explain the nature of the physiological condition that is medically diagnosed as CP, and we provide background about augmentative and alternative communication (AAC) technology. Lastly, we situate our project in the context of our collaboration and some of the methodological issues that are at stake in this type of qualitative research.

DISABILITY AS A SOCIAL PHENOMENON

Disability is a social enigma, revealing contradictory impulses within human societies. The Hebrew Bible teaches that "Thou shalt not curse the deaf nor put a stumbling block before the blind" (*Leviticus*), but also that "If you do not carefully follow His commands and decrees . . . the Lord will afflict you with madness, blindness and confusion of mind" (*Deuteronomy*) (Braddock and Parish 2001:14). Franklin Delano Roosevelt is considered by many to be one of the greatest presidents in the history of the United States, but he had to hide his polio-induced paralysis and use of a wheelchair lest the public think him too weak to lead the free world (Fleischer and Zames 2001; Holland 2006). And in daily interaction to this very day, people feel compelled both to stare at the disabled in their midst and then turn their heads in discomfort (Lenney and Sercombe 2002).

The institution of the "freak show," which reached its heyday in the nineteenth century but lasted in the United States until the 1940s and 1950s, featured people with disabilities as public spectacle. Those with physical disabilities and bodily deformities, as well as tribal nonwhite "cannibals" and "savages," were displayed for public amusement and entertainment along with sword swallowers, snake charmers, bearded women, and the full-bodied tattooed (Bogdan 1988).

The rise of a medical approach to disability, what the field of disability studies calls the *medical model*, helped change this state of affairs (Berger 2013; Siebers 2008: Williams 2001). People with disabilities were now deemed worthy of medical diagnosis and treatment and viewed more benevolently. But benevolence may breed pity, and the pitied are still stigmatized as less than full human beings. Thus the Muscular Dystrophy Association's annual telethon, which was hosted by Jerry Lewis for more than five decades, features pitiable "poster children" who help raise money for a preventative cure, but does little to improve the lives of those who are already disabled. Some may wonder why one would even want to live in such a state. As an example, the story line of Clint Eastwood's 2004 Academy Award-winning *Million Dollar Baby* went so far as to suggest that euthanasia may be the most humane response to quadriplegia (Davis 2005; Haller 2010).

In contrast, the contemporary disability rights movement advanced an alternative *social model* of disability, positing that it is not an individual's physiological impairment, but rather the socially imposed barriers—the inaccessible buildings, the limited modes of communication and transportation, the prejudicial attitudes—that construct disability as a subordinate social status and devalued life experience (Berger 2013; Oliver 1990; Shakespeare 2010; Siebers 2008). In doing so, social model proponents also advanced a critique of *ableism*, a system of oppression comparable to racism, sexism, and heterosexism that subjects people with disabilities to "political, economic, cultural, or social degradation" (Nowell 2006:1179; see also Gilson and DePoy 2000).

Ableism assumes that some people (and bodies) are "normal" and superior while other people (and bodies) are "abnormal" and inferior, and it entails institutional discrimination on the basis of this distinction. Tobin Siebers calls this the "ideology of ability," which in its simplest form constitutes a preference for able-bodiedness, but in its most radical form "defines the baseline by which humanness is determined, setting the measure of body and mind that gives or denies human status to individual persons" (2008:8). As a dominant or hegemonic ideology, ableism is so taken-for-granted that it remains unconscious and invisible to most people, even though it constitutes an overarching social regime that structures the lives of people with disabilities.

In this way, contemporary approaches to disability try to avoid the pejorative connotations of the term and reframe as a matter of social difference, or what Richard Scotch and Kay Schriner (1997) characterize as the natural variation that occurs among human beings. As Nancy Miller and Catherine Sammons argue:

> Everybody's different. Some of us have differences that no one notices, while others are different in very apparent ways. We all look different from others, sometimes by chance, sometimes by choice. Some people move on foot, while others use wheelchairs or other ways of getting around. We communicate in a variety of languages and dialects and also by using hand signs. Our behavior patterns have incredible variety, even within our own families. We all have unique physical strengths and limitations as well as different learning abilities, creative talents, and social skills. (1999:1)

Christina Papadimitriou, among others, therefore rejects a conception of disability as undesirable deviance, as a perversion of the human condition or unrelenting tragedy that propels people into depths of despair. She does not view disability and normality as polar opposites but as falling "along a continuum of . . . humanly possible ways" of being embodied in the world (2008a:219). While physiological impairments may never be wished for and are often a source of suffering (for physical and social reasons), people with disabilities differ quite dramatically in the nature of their conditions, which are not as wholly disastrous as people often imagine. They commonly learn to appreciate and enhance their remaining abilities and strive for goals and qualities of human worth that are still within their grasp (Fine and Asch 1988; Gill 2001; Potok 2002). According to Siebers, "People with disabilities want to be able to . . . live with their disability, to come to know their body, to accept what it can do, and to keep doing what they can for as long as they can. They do not want to feel dominated by people on whom they depend for help, and they want to be able to imagine themselves in a world without feeling ashamed" (2008:69). In almost every case, Siebers adds, people with disabilities have a better chance of enjoying a fulfilling life if they accept their disability as a positive aspect of their identity that provides them with a unique and at times contentious way of being embodied in the world.

Robert McRuer (2006) has extended this perspective in terms of what he calls *crip theory*, which is an effort to resignify the word crip from a pejorative to an affirmation, as well as to resignify the word *severe* as it is used to refer to those who are "severely disabled."[2] Under the regime of able-bodiedness, the severely disabled are regarded as lowest in status, especially when they are perceived as aesthetically displeasing by conventional standards. Crip theory offers a different meaning of severe as "a defiant critique, one that thoroughly and carefully reads a situation" (McRuer 2010:388). According to this view, the able-bodieds' understanding of the severely disabled is reversed: the former are deprivileged while the latter are privileged as "best positioned to call out the inadequacies of compulsory able-bodiedness" (2010:389). As Siebers argues:

> While disabled people have little power in the social world, their identities possess great theoretical power because they reflect perspectives capable of illuminating the ideological blueprints used to construct social reality. Disability identities, because of their lack of fit, serve as critical frameworks for identifying and questioning the complicated ideologies on which social injustices and oppression depend. (2008:105)

This critical perspective has been the mainstay of the independent living movement in the United States since the early 1970s, which questions able-bodied definitions of "independence" as the tasks people with disabilities can perform *without* assistance. In its stead, the independent living movement defines independence in terms of the quality of life that people with disabilities can achieve *with or without* assistance (Fleischer and Zames 2001; Shapiro 1993).

On the other hand, these "positive" views of disability have been critiqued for failing to appreciate the phenomenological experience of the body itself. According to Siebers, whereas "the medical model pays too much attention to embodiment," the social model in its purest form leaves the body out of the picture altogether (2008:25). A fuller understanding of disability, therefore, not only illuminates the effects of the social environment, but also the pains and pleasures that derive from the body itself, what Siebers calls the theory of "complex embodiment."[3] It acknowledges the chronic pain and secondary health effects that may be associated with physical impairments; that there may be available medical interventions and adaptive technologies that can improve one's quality of life; and that while environmental modifications and services can and should be available wherever possible, there are practical disadvantages to physical and cognitive impairments that no amount of environmental or social change can eliminate entirely (Bury 2000; DeJong and Basnett 2001; Shakespeare 2010; Thomas 2004). As such, for our purposes it is important for readers to be familiar with the nature of the physiological condition that is medically diagnosed as cerebral palsy.

WHAT IS CEREBRAL PALSY?

As noted previously, CP is a condition caused by trauma to the brain before, during, or shortly after birth. Congenital CP, the type that develops prior to birth, accounts for the largest proportion of cases, Jon's included. As a general medical rule of thumb, only brain injuries that occur before the age of five are referred to as CP.[4]

CP, which translates literally as "paralysis of the brain," was first described by the English orthopedic surgeon, Dr. John Little, in a paper he published in 1861. But it is Dr. William Osler, a British physician, who is believed to have been the first to coin the term "cerebral palsy" in the late 1880s. And Dr. Sigmund Freud, the Austrian neurologist who is better known for his work in psychiatry, published some of the earliest medical papers on the condition.

*Pregnancy risk factor*s for CP include conditions such as maternal diabetes or hyperthyroidism, high blood pressure, bleeding from the placenta, and premature separation of the placenta from the uterine wall. *Delivery risk factors* include breech or other fetal positions that make for a difficult delivery, prolonged rupture of the amniotic membrane that may cause fetal infection, and a severely slow fetal heart rate during labor. *Other neonatal risk factors* include asphyxia (insufficient oxygen to the brain due to breathing problems or poor blood flow to the brain), infections of the nervous system such as encephalitis and meningitis, seizures, and internal bleeding in the brain. The presence of these risk factors by no means indicates that a child will have CP. In fact, most children with these problems do not, and in those children who do have CP, it is difficult to say which of the various risk factors are implicated in any particular case.

Approximately 5 out of every 2,000 children are born with CP, with premature infants being more vulnerable than others, although 90 percent of even small premature infants do *not* have the condition. Over the recent decades, the rate of CP has remained relatively constant. On the one hand, advances in obstetrical and pediatric care have *decreased* the incidence of CP. On the other hand, these same advances have *increased* the survival rate of vulnerable premature infants.

The brain trauma that comes under the rubric of CP impairs an individual's motor functioning, with some people affected only in the lower body, some in their upper body, and some in both their lower and upper body. Some people with CP have low muscle tone, or *hypotoni*a, and some have high muscle tone, or *hypertonia*, also known as spasticity; and it is not uncommon for muscle tone to change from hypotonia to hypertonia over time. Some people may also have involuntary muscle twitching or an exaggerated startle response to external stimuli. CP may also, but not necessarily, be accompanied by neurological problems that include intellectual and learning disabilities, visual and hearing impairments, attention deficit-hyperactivity, seizures, and difficulty or inability to swallow or speak. CP is not a degenerative disease, such as Parkinson's disease or multiple sclerosis, but the normal deterioration of the body that occurs with aging can be more challenging for those with the condition.

Jon is affected in both his lower and upper body. His technical diagnosis is *athetoid* CP, also called *dyskenetic* CP, a variant of the condition that comprises about 20–25 percent of all CP cases. The condition is caused by damage to the cerebellum or basal ganglia, the areas of the brain that are responsible for maintaining body posture and smooth, coordinated movement. It may be characterized by involuntary muscle responses, and when it affects the muscles of the face and tongue, can cause grimacing and drooling and an inability to speak, the latter of which is called *dysarthria*.

As an adult, Jon uses a power wheelchair for mobility both inside and outside his home. Although he has some use of his hands, he requires assistance from either a family member or paid personal assistant for eating. Neither can Jon speak without use of an AAC device, which can be of the low tech or high tech variety. Jon did not start using a computerized device until he attended college, but today he is a proficient user of this technology, which requires him to type written commands to generate audio speech.

WHAT IS AUGMENTATIVE AND ALTERNATIVE COMMUNICATION?

AAC refers to any method of communication that relies on assistive devices to translate thought into communication. At one time only the term *augmentative* was used by professionals in the field to describe communication systems that supplemented rather than replaced verbal speech, but *alternative* was later added because some individuals use such systems as their exclusive means of communication. In either case, AAC is used by individuals with severe speech or language disabilities—an estimated 10 to 20 million people worldwide—stemming not only from CP, but also from conditions such as amyotrophic lateral sclerosis (ALS), multiple sclerosis, muscular dystrophy, Parkinson's disease, autism, and brain injury due to stroke or other trauma. The renowned physicist Stephen Hawking, who has ALS, is one of the most well-known users of AAC.[5]

Whereas *unaided* AAC includes "natural" communication such as gestures and sign language, *aided* AAC includes use of external objects such as drawings, photographs, and orthography (hand- or type-written letters or other symbols), as well as synthesized speech, or speech-generating devices (SGD), also called voice output communication aids, which use a computer algorithm that translates alphanumeric or other symbols into spoken speech. *Light tech* AAC systems include non-computer devices such as a binder or album that contains photos of common objects and familiar places and people, an alphabet display on a lap tray that can be used to point to letters to spell words, or a vest worn by a child's parents that allows the child to point to objects to communicate his or her wishes. *High tech* AAC systems use a computerized device to input messages that can be translated into audio communication.

Katya Hill and Barry Romich (2002) note that computerized AAC technology is comprised of three general elements: *selection, language representation*, and *output*. Selection entails the individual's input into the process, such as use of a keyboard, mouse, or joystick. Language representation refers to "the interface between the means of selection and the generated communication" (p. 58). Severely quadriplegic users who do not have use of their hands can activate their devices with a head or mouth stick, or a light pointer dot that is attached to their forehead that scans a computer screen attached to their wheelchairs. Nowadays users of more sophisticated systems can even activate their computer screens with the retina of their eyes; these systems use a low-intensity light source and delicate sensor to scan the blood vessels at the back of the retina.

Language-based alphabet representational methods include simple spelling, word prediction (which reduces keystrokes by anticipating the selection), and letter coding (or abbreviations); while semantic compaction, which requires more training to use proficiently, entails the use of "short sequences of symbols from a small symbol set to define words and commonly used phrases" (Hill and Romich 2002:59). Hill and Romich estimate that only a few hundred words comprise the large percentage (85–95 percent) of most people's vocabulary; and extended vocabulary, which makes up the remaining 5–15 percent of communication, consists of thousands of words. A good deal of pre-programming is often necessary to get these systems up and running. Lastly, output simply refers to the method of speech, which can be visual or audio. Depending on the sophistication of the system, the audio output can sound either robotic or natural.

Learning to use high-tech SGDs takes a good deal of time and practice, and speech output for even the most proficient user is much slower than ordinary speech. Jon currently uses a keyboard to generate audio speech on an SGD that he did not start using until he attended college, and we estimate that he can type, on average, 10 to 12 words a minute. There are some individuals who can type faster than Jon, but most users are able to type no more than 10 words a minute, at best. Jan Bedrosian and colleagues (1998) estimate that the average speaker without a communicative disability speaks at a rate about seven times faster than a high-end SGD user.

THE CONTEXT OF OUR COLLABORATION

Our project began organically, at Jon's behest, not as a preconceived research study. The entire process was thus marked by an inductive logic that is characteristic of much qualitative research, where the initial research problem was "a starting point for inquiry rather than an end point of research design" (Charmaz 2012:128; Clandinin 2013).[6] As such, our methodological approach evolved over time and was constituted by a "mixed methods" strategy that included Jon's own written narrative, interviews by Ron and Jennifer with Jon and significant others, and participant observation by Ron in various social milieus. Although it is commonly assumed that mixed methods must involve both qualitative and quantitative methods, Kathy Charmaz calls for "expanding conceptions of mixed methods to include different forms of qualitative research in the same project" and using mixed methods "to create a finished product that shows that the whole is greater than would be gained by only using separate methods" (2011:126, 131).

The precipitating occasion for Jon's initial contact with Ron was a collaborative book Ron had published with Melvin Juette called *Wheelchair Warrior: Gangs, Disability and Basketball* (Juette and Berger 2008). Melvin had grown up in Chicago where he had become involved in the city's notorious street gang scene. In 1986, at the age of 16, he was shot and paralyzed, a dramatic event that caused him to change his life. He became involved in wheelchair basketball and later enrolled at the University of Wisconsin-Whitewater (UWW) to play on its collegiate wheelchair basketball team. Melvin eventually went on to become the first UWW student to play on the U.S. national team in the international Paralympics and Gold Cup, and he became a role model to other students with disabilities.

Melvin had been one of Ron's students, and though Jon was not a student of Ron's, he had received a bachelor's degree in psychology and a master's degree in special education from UWW. As such, in both Melvin's and Jon's case, the organic context of their collaboration with Ron was their mutual embeddedness in a university that has as its special mission within the University of Wisconsin System the provision of services to students with disabilities. UWW is a completely accessible campus and has a Center for Students with Disabilities (CSD), formerly called Disabled Student Services (DSS), which offers a number of specialized services, including academic and career counseling, instructional aids, technology and transportation assistance, liaison with government and community agencies, and recreational and sports opportunities. Currently CSD serves about 700 students a year, about 6 percent of the UWW student body.

This is the context in which our lives came together when Jon approached Ron about helping him write his autobiography. During the summer of 2003, after obtaining his bachelor's degree and starting his master's degree, Jon had read two autobiographies of successful people with CP: Bill Rush's *Journey Out of Silence* (1986) and Rick Creech's *Reflections from a Unicorn* (1992). Both of these writers had gone on to college and, as Jon's father would say, "made a life for themselves." Now Jon, who was also making a life for himself, wanted to tell his story too. By his own admission, Jon has a big enough ego to think that *his* story merited telling. He was proud of having earned his college degrees and of self-publishing two books: *Straight Talks*

(2004), a book of his speeches, and *The Tan Car* (2003b), a book of his poems. And he is the founding director of Authentic Voices of America (AVA), an innovative summer camp for young people with disabilities who are learning to use or become more proficient at using computerized technologies to speak. To our knowledge, AVA is the first of such camps in the United States (and presumably the world) to be run by an actual SGD user.

At the same time, Jon had enough self-awareness of his limitations as a writer to know that he did not have enough skill to write a publisher-sponsored book on his own. Of Ron, Jon said, "I really wanted to meet this guy and see if he would be interested in helping me. I was very intrigued because over the last few years he was emerging on campus as a person getting into disability studies."

"The text of a written biography," Ann Oakley observes, "is the product of two biographies—the writer and the person written about," and all biographical writers must ask themselves the question, "am I the right person to do this biography?" (2010:431). In our case, however, it was Jon who asked the question, of Ron and Jennifer, "are they the right persons to help me write my story?" Thus after learning about the publication of *Wheelchair Warrior*, Jon sent Ron an e-mail expressing his interest in setting up a meeting to discuss the possibility of collaborating on a book about his life.

The meeting between Jon and Ron was arranged, and when Jon arrived in Ron's campus office, Ron felt as if Jon was interviewing him for a job. Jon wanted to make sure he was comfortable with Ron; and if they both agreed to the project, that Ron would be committed to following through.

People with disabilities are often skeptical of able-bodied researchers, feeling that they might lack empathy and be unduly influenced by able-bodied assumptions (Akamanti 2004; Branfield 1998; Charlton 1998; Oliver 1992). Ron is an able-bodied man, but he has familial experience with disability (his daughter has a relatively moderate case of CP), and his previous collaborative research with Melvin and his involvement in teaching a course on disability—to say nothing of his professional publishing record—gave him some credibility in Jon's eyes.

Jon explained to Ron that he was a little disgruntled that wheelchair athletes like Melvin seemed to get all of the attention and notoriety. He said he did not even think that Melvin, who uses a manual wheelchair for mobility and who has no physical impairment above his hips, was even disabled. Jon said he thought it was important to tell a story about someone, like himself, who is "really disabled."

Interestingly, Jon's complaint raised the question of *authenticity*, an issue that is prominent in the disability community and academic disability studies: Who can lay claim to speak for or legitimately represent the disability experience? In one case that received national attention in 2005, for example, Janeal Lee was forced to forfeit her crown and the prizes she received for being selected as the Wisconsin representative to the national Ms. Wheelchair America (MWA) contest (Peters 2005). The national organization, which oversees the individual state contests, ruled that Lee was ineligible because she was not sufficiently disabled. Lee, a high school math teacher, has a progressive form of muscular dystrophy. She uses a wheelchair for mobility and can only stand for about 10 to 15 minutes without tiring. She does walk around her classroom, however, holding onto a chair or desk for stability. When MWA organizers saw a picture in a local newspaper of Lee standing, they declared her insufficiently disabled to compete. According to the organizers, MWA rules required a valid contestant to "utilize a wheelchair for daily mobility."

Similarly, Mark Deal (2003) reports that young men with muscle-wasting impairments due to muscular dystrophy felt animosity toward those who were able to maximize their upper-body strength to play wheelchair sports. And in Ron's broader study of the UWW wheelchair basketball program (beyond his work with Melvin), he found a division between disabled students who played basketball and those who did not, whereby some nonplaying students thought that the athletes were snobbish and elitist, while some athletes felt that students who used power wheelchairs were lazy (Berger 2009). Thus Ruth Galvin (2003) observes that people with disabilities have created their own divisive identifications that undermine cross-disability or pan-disability consciousness. It is noteworthy that Jon now says he regrets making the comment about Melvin, not wanting to fall into the trap of engaging in what Lennard Davis calls "policing action" regarding authentic or inauthentic disabilities that can turn on itself and reproduce the same hierarchical patterns of inclusion and exclusion that people with disabilities have been fighting against (2001:538).

Be that as it may, given Ron's other commitments at the time, he told Jon that he would be interested in helping him if Jon could write the bulk of his autobiographical narrative on his own. They also talked about including interviews with people whose knowledge of Jon might enhance the story. Jon agreed to this arrangement, but as the subsequent months passed, after writing about 20 pages of narrative covering the early part of his life, he hit a wall. At the time Jon admitted he had been suffering from depression and no longer felt he could write on his own (Ellensen 2005), and he asked Ron if he would be willing to meet regularly with him to record his story. Later Jon would discover that he was suffering from bipolar disorder and had not been properly diagnosed and treated with the appropriate medication.

At this point in our collaboration this was not a time commitment Ron was able to make. But he told Jon he would explore the possibility of getting someone else involved in the project, either a student or another faculty member. Ron contacted his colleague Jennifer Flad, who expressed an interest in the collaboration. Ron told Jon about Jennifer's background as an

experienced and emphatic ethnographer and interviewer, with a specializa-
tion in medical sociology. He also assured Jon that he would like her very
much as a person. Jon was enthusiastic about meeting her, and we set up a
meeting with the three of us.

When Jennifer first contemplated the idea of a life history project of this
nature, she had serious reservations. Previously when she had taken a methodology course in graduate school on life history and narratives, she had been
intrigued by the detail and knowledge that could be produced by a researcher
working with a key informant. At the same time, she was struck by the
unequal power dynamics that she consistently witnessed as she read the
words of the informants but saw the researchers' names on the articles or
books that were published. This struck her as rather exploitative, and she
voiced her concern to her professor, who himself was engaged in this type of
work. His response was to challenge her to think through her methodological
choices: whether she really wanted to conduct qualitative interviews and
advance her own professional career by doing such work.

Jennifer's struggles with how to produce knowledge with informants led
her to investigate other methods of inquiry. She found feminist sources that
addressed these concerns, and the perspective she gained solidified her
stance on research committed to evaluating epistemology and the need for
self-reflexive inquiry; and she became increasingly attracted to research that
treated informants as true experts of their own experience. If power was
inherent in all forms of research with human subjects, then such reflexivity
becomes necessary to unpack what knowledge is contingent upon and how
the researcher and research process are socially situated and organized (Ramazanoglu and Holland 2002; Reinharz 1992).

In his own work, too, Ron had grappled with this dilemma and felt he had
resolved it to his satisfaction. In undertaking his work with Melvin and other
wheelchair athletes, he had viewed the project as a joint production between
himself and the research participants, only interviewing people who wanted
their stories to be told (Berger 2009; Juette and Berger 2008). His goal had
been to tap into the tacit knowledge available to insiders of a social milieu, to
learn from them rather than to *study* them. In doing so, he had also hoped to
gain insight into his daughter's experience of disability.

In disability studies, especially in Great Britain, this approach is often
referred to as "emancipatory research." According to Mike Oliver, "one cannot 'do' emancipatory research (nor write methodology cookbooks on how to
do it), one can only engage as a researcher with those seeking to emancipate
themselves" (1997:25; see also Oliver 1992; Zarb 1992). What this means
more precisely is subject to some dispute. While some have defined this
approach somewhat narrowly, essentially equating it with participatory research in the context of progressive political action for people with disabilities,[7] others suggest that the very act of telling one's story may be empower-

ing in and of itself (Petersen 2011). Elsewhere we have referred to this process as a matter of "methodological empowerment" (Flad, Berger, and Feucht 2011). At the same time, some scholars with disabilities believe that nondisabled people are ideologically incapable of engaging in emancipatory research, thinking they should stay out of disability studies altogether (Branfield 1998; Charlton 1998). Rob Kitchin (2000), for one, disagrees, thinking it is unwise to leave the field in the hands of a small cadre of academics with disabilities who may have agendas of their own that do not represent the interests of the diverse constituency of disabled people. All that is necessary, Kitchin argues, is that researchers approach their topics from a "disabled-friendly" point of view (p. 36). In this way, as Robert Whittemore and colleagues (1986) observe, the experiential expertise of the disabled participant and the analytical and reportorial skills of the researcher (disabled or nondisabled) combine to draw out broader social, cultural, and political issues (see also Akamanti 2004; Darling 2000; Duckett 1998).

All too often scholarly discussions of emancipatory and feminist-oriented research take place without acknowledgment of a broader interdisciplinary trend in qualitative inquiry, loosely characterized as imbued with a postmodern sensibility, which eschews the idea of the trained "social science voyeur" who stands apart from the experience being observed, remembered, or recorded (Berger and Quinney 2005; Clandinin 2013; Denzin 1998:411). In this interdisciplinary tradition there is an ongoing effort to guard against exploiting informants for the purpose of professional aggrandizement, and an awareness that a researcher's "primary obligation is always to the people [they] study," not to their project or discipline (Denzin 1989:83). Researchers are viewed as engaged in a process of collaboration with informants who retain some degree of control over the research agenda, at least with respect to what gets said or not said; and they are expected to engage in a process of ongoing self-reflection to clear themselves of personal and professional biases that may interfere with their ability to hear and empathize with others (Ellis and Rawicki 2013; Flad, Berger, and Feucht 2011; Papadimitriou 2001; Petersen 2011).

When Jennifer met Jon for the first time, she too felt like she was being interviewed for a job. As she sat in Ron's office waiting to meet Jon, she was nervous and hoped she would appear to him as someone who could be trusted. When Jon arrived, Ron introduced him to Jennifer, and after a little small talk, Jon discussed his hopes for the project. He was disappointed and frustrated that he had not been able to make more progress writing his story on his own. Jennifer's role would be to work with him on a regular basis to help him tell it. Using a loosely-structured chronological framework, they would attempt to document Jon's life story and flush out details of thought and action relevant to his experience of disability.

Jennifer was immediately put at ease by the meeting. Foremost in her mind was that it was Jon who wanted to tell his story and that he would be calling the shots and seemed to know what he wanted to say. She felt that any exploitation she had anticipated was at least minimized by this encounter and the premise of the project: Jon was and would remain an active participant and co-producer of the knowledge we would create together.

EMERGENT ISSUES

As noted, our methodological approach to documenting Jon's life evolved over time in the course of our work, and the initial interviews that Jennifer conducted with Jon raised some unanticipated issues. Their initial sessions took place in Jennifer's campus office; Jon arrived, and before they knew it an hour and a half went by. Utilizing Jon's computerized device for an interview was great in some ways. Jon was able to plug his device into Jennifer's computer and whatever he typed would open into a Word document. They learned how to negotiate this protocol as they went along. Jon, for instance, wanted to be able to make sure that his words were being recorded correctly on the screen, and that when he deleted or changed a word, it changed as he desired. He also wanted Jennifer to type any questions and follow-up questions that she asked of him, so he could view them on the screen—both so that he could carefully choose his words for his response and also simply "for the record."

Jon felt that he and Jennifer "clicked right away, getting things written and showing everybody involved that we're on our way to producing something special." He said that the "addition of Jennifer was the missing piece in the puzzle" in getting the project going.

Although Jon had been frustrated with his own contribution to the project, he was highly motivated to get his story "out there." During the first couple of sessions and in e-mail correspondences, Jon repeatedly asked Jennifer if she was in it for the "long haul," because the amount of data that would be needed to generate a book would take a considerable period of time. Thus the two of them began structuring their time together in ways that enabled them to complete as much interview work in each session as possible.

In an average 60–90 minute session, Jon and Jennifer were only able to produce from one paragraph to about a half page of dialogue. The time that this took, even with the automatic transcription, was for Jennifer a new dimension of the interview process. They quickly learned to "get right into it" when Jon arrived in order to preserve their time together, and in doing so found themselves cutting out the "small talk"—the niceties that come with a growing relationship. But this was problematic for Jennifer, a disjuncture from her previous interview experiences, especially interviews around the sort of intimate and personal aspects of one's life that she had explored with others and was now doing with Jon. Thus when Jon came in sniffling one day, Jennifer's response was to ask him about his health. This took up about 10 minutes of their time. Consequently, Jennifer learned to choose her words carefully about "non-work" matters so that Jon would not feel the need to respond. They would devote as much time as they could for the work, and when their time was up, Jon would abruptly leave the room. Jennifer was disappointed that she did not get to ask Jon how his wife was or whether he was doing anything special over the weekend. For her, this was not simply "small talk," but a way for her to show Jon that she cared about him and was interested in him as a person, not simply as someone she was interviewing for a research project.

At first, Jennifer thought that Jon was a little skeptical of her intentions or of their ability to work well together, and they had to work through a process of establishing trust and intersubjective understanding, which is arguably one of the most challenging aspects of research between nondisabled researchers and disabled informants. With the limited time available for each session, Jennifer had to compose the questions she wanted to ask carefully, limiting herself to one or two each session, and it became frustrating to both of them when she would ask something that was unclear or when one or both of them couldn't figure out what the other was trying to say. Of course, language barriers exist with everyone who tries to express themselves to others, and we are often misunderstood. But to Jennifer the potential for misunderstanding with Jon seemed more complex and challenging. Sometimes Jon didn't feel that she really understood his meaning, and they spent the majority of their time straightening this out. At the same time, these encounters were "teachable moments," as Jennifer began reflecting upon her own tendency to speak quickly without thinking through the clarity of what she was saying, and also about some of her own biases or preconceived notions about people with disabilities. Papadimitriou describes this element of the disability research process in phenomenological terms as entailing "two movements: one reflexive the other emphatic" (2001:48). In the reflexive mode the researcher looks within in order to bracket or "clear oneself out of the way," and in the emphatic mode s/he looks "outward to the world of disability in order to listen to the Other's experience."[8]

One of the problematic encounters between Jennifer and Jon involved a discussion about what Jon described as two kinds of students at UWW: those who tend to stay at home and don't "get off their behinds," and those like Jon who are advocates for themselves and actively engage their community in an effort "to make their mark on the world" (Feucht 2003a). Jennifer was taken aback by Jon's critical view of the former group of students, especially in light of Jon's accounts of the discriminatory barriers he has faced in his life. She asked him why he thought the first group of students behaved in the way that they did. Perhaps this was their mode of adaptation to the very same structural barriers that Jon himself had encountered.

Jon seemed to take some offense at this and wanted to set Jennifer straight. He insisted that we should not blame anything on outside forces—that the struggles he has endured would be like a catcher saying he could not deal with the fastballs coming at him or like a smoker who blames getting cancer on the tobacco company. In sociological terms, it became apparent that Jon was privileging *personal agency* over *social structure* in his view of the world, whereas Jennifer was privileging structure over agency. Ron, too, had encountered this view among some of the disabled wheelchair athletes he had interviewed in his previous research, with some who told him that "there are some people who try to use their disability to their advantage" by asking for accommodations they don't need, or "who have the ability . . . [but] they just let other people help them all the time." As one informant who was born without legs explained, "Whitewater has created a wonderful little Disney World for people with disabilities. They do everything for them. . . . [Today, people with disabilities have rights, but] the biggest problem with that fact is that once you get the rights, the hardest thing to do is to encourage people to use those rights" (Berger 2009: 66, 76, 88).

Jennifer began wondering whether her emphasis on structure, so common among sociologists, reflected an ableist bias that lowered expectations for people with disabilities.[9] She realized that the story Jon wanted to tell was not a story about structural barriers, but about refusing to give in to lowered expectations and about working hard to improve oneself and be a role model for others: to be the best you can be, and to get the tools you need to do that.

Be that as it may, any adequate sociological interpretation of any social phenomenon, disability or otherwise, needs to take into account both personal agency and social structure—and the dynamic interplay between the two—for these are the two foundational categories of *all* sociological discourse (Alexander 1982; Giddens 1984). The problem with much life history research, as Ron has elsewhere pointed out, is that researchers have under-theorized the link, failing to note that both agency and structure each presuppose the other and are simultaneously enacted in specific situational contexts (Berger 2008a). In doing so, they also fail to illuminate the ways in which agentive action is not simply *constrained* by social structure but also *enabled* by it, facilitating the ongoing transformation of social structures and hence social change (Giddens 1984; Sewell 1992). In the case of disability, for example, the ability of agentive actors to transform social structures that constrain the lives of people with disabilities has been enabled by the contemporary disability rights movement, of which Jon is a part, as well as advances in assistive technology. At the same time, people like Jon inarguably possess the quality of what social psychologists describe as a self-efficacy, and which Jon describes as a matter of self-determination, that is, the ability to experience oneself as a causal agent capable of *acting upon* rather than merely *reacting* to their external environment (Bandura 1997; Gecas 1989; Wehmeyer and Field 2007).

Committing ourselves to an epistemological stance of co-producing knowledge, while also maintaining a posture of mutual self-reflexivity, required an ongoing assessment of the process of research production. And focusing on Jon's expert knowledge of his experience, while also engaging him in conversations about sociological and methodological issues, required a working relationship of open communication and open-mindedness. During the course of our research, the three of us opened up an ongoing discussion about our experience of doing this work and of our mutual goals for the project. In doing so, a more personal relationship between us emerged. It was also at this point that we began to realize that Jon's initial desire to pen his autobiography was evolving into a broader qualitative research project.

After about a year of periodic interviews with Jon, Jennifer gave birth to her first child, and the demands (and rewards) of raising an infant necessitated a reduced role in the project. By this time, however, Ron was able to return to a fuller engagement with the data collection and began conducting a series of interviews with Jon on his own. Eschewing the computerized approach that Jennifer had used with Jon, Ron found it less cumbersome to simply write down Jon's remarks by hand, which was easy to do because of the relatively slow pace of Jon's communication. In doing so, Ron became aware that there are two ways in which Jon speaks. In one way Jon allows the audio to play as he types each and every word—including errors and corrected errors—before playing back the entire paragraph. In the second way, Jon withholds his audio input until he has completed the entirety of his thoughts. When Jon used the first method of output, it was easy for Ron to record his communication.

During this time of our collaboration, Jon was diagnosed with bipolar disorder, and with the proper medication, began writing again on his own. Ron also interviewed Jon's parents (Janet and Al), the communication specialist who introduced Jon to his first SGD in college (Connie Wiersma), and one of his professors who had spoken at an AVA camp (Dr. David Travis). Jon's older siblings (Janeen and Jeff) also provided written narratives of their recollections growing up with their younger brother. Additionally, Ron had the opportunity to visit Jon and his wife Sarah in their home, attend a week-long AVA summer camp held on the UWW campus in 2011, and travel with Jon and Sarah to a professional conference in 2012, which was attended by Jennifer as well. These venues afforded opportunities for Ron, as a participant observer, to immerse himself in the phenomenological world of significantly disabled people. As a result of these experiences, Ron and Jon developed a close friendship, a further reward of conducting this type of research (Tillmann-Healy 2003). Although the conventional methodological posture cautions against the loss of analytic detachment, postmodern approaches encourage a "relational methodology," whereby we "intentionally put our lives alongside an other's life" (Clandinin 2013:23) and adopt "an approach to a community, setting, group, issue, or category of people in which the researcher has a sustained involvement in the studied world" (Charmaz 2012:130).

NOTES

1. As an example, see Dan Goodley's chapter on "sociological disability studies" in *Disability Studies: An Interdisciplinary Introduction* (2011).

2. Crip theory entails an adaptation of concepts from feminist and queer theory. For more on the relationship between these theoretical traditions, see Berger (2013); Goodley (2011); Sherry (2004).

3. Within disability studies, this debate implicates a distinction that is often made between "impairment" and "disability," with the former referring to a biological or physiological condition that entails the loss of physical, sensory, or cognitive function, and the latter referring to an inability to perform a personal or socially necessary task because of that impairment or the societal reaction to it (Berger 2013; Goodley 2011). At the same time, as Bill Hughes and Kevin Paterson observe, the distinction between impairment and disability is difficult to maintain; they do not "meet in the body . . . as a dualistic clash of inner and outer phenomena" but are mutually constituted and fully integrated in an embodied whole (1997:335).

4. This section on CP is derived from the following sources: Cerebral Palsy Source (2013); Geralis (1991); Hou, Yu, and Zhao (2006); Jones, Morgan, and Shelton (2007); Miller and Bachrach (1995).

5. This section on augmentative and alternative communication is derived from the following sources: AAC Mentor Project (2010); Baker (2005); Beukelman and Mirenda (2012); Brownlee (n.d.); Glennen (1997); Higgenbotham et al. (2007); Hill and Romich (2002); Jans and Clark (1998); Schlosser, Blischak, and Koul (2003); Sigafoos and Drasgow (2001); Vanderheide (2002).

6. Inductive methodology is often framed in terms of Barry Glaser and Anselm Strauss's (1967) "grounded theory" approach, but these scholars were interested in the development of abstract theoretical propositions not in the illumination of lived experience.

7. More generally, outside of disability studies this method is called action research and participatory action research (Cassell and Johnson 2006; Stoecker 1999).

8. For an inquiry into the concept of "Othering," see Krumer-Nevo (2012).

9. As an example of lower expectations, Joan Tollifson (1997), who is missing her right hand and half of her right arm, writes about how people would be amazed that she could perform such mundane tasks as tying her own shoe.

Part 1

The Life History

Chapter Two

Growing Up with Cerebral Palsy

Life history research, also called interpretive biography and life story research, is a time-honored tradition in sociology that has "vacillated in acceptance and popularity over the years" (Goetting 1995:5).[1] For us it is a methodological choice well suited to illuminating the experience of individuals in social context and in particular the experience of disability in society. Over the next three chapters, we tell Jon's story in chronological fashion, beginning with his childhood and through his college years, involvement in Authentic Voices of America, and marriage. As such, we follow his movement across the life course, which may be defined as an age-graded sequence of socially defined roles that individuals enact over time as they exercise agency in the context of structural constraints and opportunities (Elder 1995).

Ann Goetting argues that biography is "not simply a 'true' representation of an objective 'reality,'" but an incomplete reconstruction of a remembered past that is inevitably marked by a degree of distortion because of the fallibility of memory and the subjectivity of perception (1995:13). If a person's story is told honestly, to the best of his or her ability, it may be the closest approximation to the truth he or she can muster, but it is not the invariant "truth" of what transpired. At the same time, *how one remembers* the past may be the most essentially part of *the story* he or she has to tell (Goetting 1995; Gusdorf 1980). As Robert Atkinson observes, "a person's story is essentially an expression of his or her self-understanding. . . . What may be of greatest interest . . . is how [they] see themselves and . . . want others to see them" (1998:20).

In fashioning the disparate elements of Jon's story, we also began thinking about the nature of its narrative trajectory or arc. Storytelling is about life events that are imbued with a temporal and logical order, that establish continuity between the past, present—and if the story is not yet finished—an unrealized future, and that transform human experience into meaning (Ochs and Capps 2001). It turns mere chronology—one thing after another—into "the purposeful action of plot" (Taylor 2001:2). A coherent plot is one that has a beginning, middle, and end; it grows plausibly out of what has come before and points the way to what might reasonably come next. Hayden White calls this *emplotment*, the way in which "a sequence of events fashioned into a story is gradually revealed to be a story of a particular kind" (1973:7).[2]

Storytelling also involves appropriation of general narrative formats, conventions, and archetypal experiences that structure how people tell and write about lives (Bruner 2004; Clandinin 2013; Taylor 2001). Typically such stories, if they are compelling stories, are marked by key turning points or epiphanies in which protagonists take agentive actions in the face of adversity, falter and progress, and (in stories with happy endings) ultimately triumph. Often they are framed in terms of what Arthur Frank (1995) calls the archetypal "quest" narrative, in the case of disability, a story about rising to the occasion and refusing to give in to despair in order to reach a desired goal.

Insofar as Jon's story can be framed as a quest, it is his desire to achieve his share of the American dream, a dream that is denied to all too many people with disabilities, especially to those whose disabilities are as significant as Jon's. The idea of the "American dream," first introduced into contemporary social discourse by historian James Truslow Adams (1931), described a vision of a society that was open to individual achievement. While this vision came to take on a narrow meaning that equated it with the acquisition of financial success,[3] others view the dream in terms of the opportunity for self-fulfillment, which includes material comforts but also seeks a higher calling, in Abraham Maslow's (1954) terms, the opportunity to become a self-actualized human being, and to be recognized as such by others. Most importantly, for Jon, it means moving beyond the low expectations that society has for people with disabilities and achieving what he calls the "tripod of success," that is, "the ability to get your life in sync across the board—in your home life, education, and occupation."

There have been times, however, when Jon experienced his life less as a quest than as a life filled with chaos, what John Barth describes as having a plot that "doesn't progress by meaningful steps, but winds upon itself, digresses, retreats" (1968:96). As David Carr observes, "Our lives admit of sometimes more, sometimes less coherence; they hang together reasonably well, but they occasionally tend to fall apart. . . . The unity of self, not as an underlying identity but as a life that hangs together, is not a pregiven condition but an achievement" (1986:97).

Up until Jon was treated for his bipolar condition, which did not occur until he was in his thirties, Jon's life could be described as a quest interspersed with chaos. Even so, there was always unstoppable forward movement: graduation from high school, undergraduate and graduate college degrees, Authentic Voices of America, and marriage. At the same time, for Jon there is always another mountain to climb, another obstacle to be overcome, another goal to be achieved. He is never at rest, never satisfied with resting on his accomplishments, never thinking it is enough, always struggling to live up to other's admiration for what he has achieved thus far.

Jon was born at St. Agnes Hospital in Fond du Lac, Wisconsin, in 1977, and grew up in small towns in the southeastern part of the state. His parents, Janet and Al, remember him as a colicky baby, crying constantly, from morning until night. He might fall asleep for 20 minutes at a time, giving them only a brief respite. For the first few years of Jon's life, he shared a bedroom with his sister Janeen, who was three years older, who at times would push his crib into the hallway at night so she could try and get some sleep. She even threatened to run away to live with the neighbors because his crying was so hard to bear.

Janet and Al became particularly concerned when they noticed that Jon was not swallowing his milk, and they thought he might have a milk allergy. After consulting with their pediatrician, Jon was put on soy milk, but Janet and Al soon realized he also had a problem with swallowing. Jon was prescribed medications to relax him, as many as five different kinds over a period of time, but he also experienced other symptoms. He'd throw his head back and stiffen his body, his hands seemed unusually curled, and he wasn't crawling or communicating verbally.

Janet and Al began worrying that something serious was wrong. They got a referral to see Dr. Irene Ibler at the Waisman Center in Madison. An affiliate of the University of Wisconsin Hospital, the Waisman Center is a specialty clinic involved in research and treatment of children with developmental disabilities. It was there that Dr. Ibler diagnosed Jon as having cerebral palsy. Janet and Al were baffled. How could this have happened? Janet had done everything right. She had been careful about what she had eaten and had not smoked or drank alcohol. There must be some reason for this, she kept insisting.

CP may be caused by any number of factors (see chapter 1), but in Jon's case the prevailing theory implicates his father's exposure to Agent Orange during his service in the Vietnam War (see Erickson 1997; King 2012; Mekdeci 2007). At the time of his diagnosis, exposure to Agent Orange, a dioxin-contaminated chemical, was just starting to be linked to birth defects. Jon's father asked Dr. Ibler if this could be the cause, but she was reluctant to be too definitive. "Don't ever go there." she said. "If you try to prove that, you'll get raked over the coals."

Janet and Al started putting two plus two together. Their oldest Jeff, born in 1967, is perfectly healthy, but he was born just after Al was sent to Vietnam. Their daughter Janeen, born in 1974, seemed fine at birth, but she began suffering from degenerative arthritis in her early teens. In between, in 1970, Janet gave birth to a still-born child. There seemed to be a pattern here.

A few years after Jon's diagnosis, upon her retirement, Dr. Ibler told Janet and Al there was no doubt in her mind that Agent Orange was the cause of his CP. But earlier, she said, she had not wanted them to get involved in pursuing what she thought would be a time-consuming and potentially fruitless grievance against the federal government to try to get some kind of compensation for what happened. In any case, Janet and Al are not the type of people who would have wanted to pursue such a case. Their attitude was, "the damage is already done, this is not about money."

When Jon was first diagnosed with CP, Janet and Al did not know how significant a case he would have. Although CP is a common diagnostic term, it glosses over a wide range of impairments, the particular manifestation of which depends on the part or parts of the brain that are affected. If someone would look at Jon today, they would likely perceive him as a severely disabled man. He has what in medical parlance is called athetoid CP, and all four of his limbs are affected. He relies on a power chair for mobility, maneuvering his chair by manipulating a joystick with the fingers of his left hand. Sometimes when he gets frustrated or excited, his arms will flail about in the air and he may bounce a little out of his seat. He may appear to breathe heavily, and once in a while have a little saliva secrete from his mouth. Jon is unable to feed himself, but he can shower, dress, and toilet himself on his own. Arguably the most notable thing about his disability is that he cannot speak without the use of an augmentative communication device. It is this element of his condition that has become the defining feature of his disability. In many ways, however, unlike the way other people see him, Jon views himself as only moderately disabled. As he says:

There are many other people who have more severe disabilities than me. Everything is relative, I suppose. I have, through great determination, perseverance, and the support of my family, accomplished a great deal in my life. My parents never thought I'd be able to go to college, but I've earned my bachelor's and master's degrees, and I'm currently working on a doctorate in educational leadership and public policy. I am the founding director of Authentic Voices of America, a summer camp for young people with disabilities who are learning to use augmentative communication. I have self-published two books and am now the coauthor of the book you are reading about my life. I do not have any regrets or misgivings about having cerebral palsy. I have lived with this condition my entire life. It is who I am, and it has given me special insights into living with a disability in a world constructed for nondisabled people. I want you to get to know me, to help you know others like me and what they might become if they were able to access the opportunities I've had and learn how to negotiate a world that is still not fully accepting of people with disabilities.

Research on families and childhood disability finds that it is common for parents to feel guilty about what transpired, thinking they must have done something wrong (Landsman 2009; Marshak, Seligman, and Prezant 1999; Naseef 2001; Solomon 2012). Or they might feel self-pity, thinking, "Why us? What did we do to deserve this?" Jon's parents experienced both of these emotions. Research also finds that whereas mothers tend to be more concerned with their ability to cope with childcare responsibilities, fathers tend to be more concerned about the prospects of their child—especially their sons—adopting socially acceptable behaviors, participating in sports, and enjoying occupational success. Jon's father tended to react stoically upon hearing the news of Jon's CP, while his mother recalls returning from the Waisman Center crying and saying, "My life is over." As Jon observes:

> There is some truth to this, because her life as she knew it was indeed over. For the first 19 years of my life, while my dad was working, my mom took care of all my basic needs, for which I need assistance. She got me up every morning, helped me get dressed, fed me my breakfast, and put me on the bus for school. She'd be waiting for me when I returned from school, made sure I did my homework, fed me my supper, and got me ready for bed.
>
> I admit, too, that my mom and I locked horns and argued many a time over the years. This is not because we were different but because we were so much alike—stubborn and strong-willed. Often my dad would come home from work and for the first five minutes he'd have to play referee. But I have nothing but admiration for my parents' dedication to me and our entire family. They sacrificed a lot for my brother, sister, and me, rarely having time for themselves, and they were always exhausted. They were, I should say *are*, hard-working, success-driven people, and I'm sure I get much of my drive to succeed from them.

During Jon's youth, his family lived in three different homes, the first in the rural community of LeRoy, a small town with a population of about 1,000, and the other two in the nearby "big city" of Waupun, which had a population of about 8,200. He remembers being unhappy with the move to the first home in Waupun, which his parents chose because they wanted him to attend an elementary school in that district where they thought he would receive more attention. The Feucht family seemed to be living on top of each other, and there was no privacy. Jon had his own bedroom that he could crawl to on this own, but it was a converted den with a translucent fireplace that did double-duty in the living room. Often, when he was trying to sleep and the others were watching television in the living room, his room would light up like a Christmas tree.

Living under these conditions created a lot of tension. There were many times when two of them would be arguing, but when somebody else came into the room, they would turn on them. To break up the tension, Al and Jon would periodically designate a week as "prank week." Al's morning routine at the time was to come into Jon's bedroom at 4:00 a.m. to make sure he was covered up before he left for work. One time, Jon recalls, he felt his father adjusting something under his pillow. Jon thought to himself, "What is he doing?" and discovered that his father had put a pair of dirty underwear under his pillow. It was a silly kind of prank, but Jon loved it and thought, "Game on . . . I retaliated by toilet papering my parents' bedroom. My mom eventually put a stop to it before we destroyed the house."

Until Jon was eight years old, his father worked as a meat cutter in a meat market in LeRoy, but in 1985 Al and Janet purchased a meat market of their own, Brandon Meats, in the neighboring small town of Brandon. Al worked very long hours, and by the time he got home all he wanted to do was sleep. In many ways Jon felt deprived of his attention, but they still did a lot of things together as a family. They went to places like Great America, where having a wheelchair was an advantage because Jon got to go to the front of the line. He particularly remembers a couple of summers when they would rent a cabin on the lake and enjoy a week of swimming and fishing.

Brandon Meats was the financial backbone of the Feucht family, and it eventually allowed Al and Janet to purchase a larger home in Waupun when Jon was 16 years old, as well as a camping trailer and boat for the family to enjoy. "I never lacked for anything I needed," Jon says, "and my family's financial stability and the support they have given me to this very day cannot be underestimated. Outside of my own drive, determination and will to per- severe, I have not had to worry about financial matters." Unfortunately, the same cannot be said for so many other people with disabilities, who are disproportionately represented among the ranks of the poor in both the Unit- ed States and around the world (Barnes and Sheldon 2010; Charlton 1998; Schriner 2001; Stodden and Dowrick 2000).

Like many children, Jon does not think he appreciated his parents as much as he does today. There were times when he acted out to get their attention, and he had a lot of problems with anger management. It was not until he was in his mid-thirties that he was finally diagnosed and treated for bipolar disorder. Prior to that time he also suffered from depression, and he was diagnosed, or now thinks misdiagnosed, as having a generalized anxiety disorder. Given what Jon now knows about bipolar disorder, he suspects he was given the wrong medications that only made his problems worse. Even though he was in counseling for years, beginning in his adolescence, the therapists he saw never got to the root of the problem. In all fairness to these professionals, bipolar disorder was not on the "radar screen" of the field as much as it is today; and the symptoms of mania—extreme highs and lows—are often correlated with depression.[4] In retrospect, Jon says, "I blame them for not properly diagnosing me, but I also blame myself for holding back, for not telling the truth about what I was feeling, for masking my insecurities and conflict with my parents. I had enough going against me with my physical disabilities that I didn't want to be labeled as having a mental disability too."

Two years before Jon was born, the U.S. Congress passed the Education for All Handicapped Children Act (EAHCA), reauthorized and amended in the Individuals with Disabilities Education Act in 1990, guaranteeing a free public education to children with disabilities, along with appropriate accommodations and special education services (Fleischer and Zames 2001; Marshak, Seligman, and Prezant 1999). In an amendment passed in 1986, it also created the Early Intervention Program, which provides services to children under the age of three who have been identified as having a developmental disability (Leiter 2007). But Jon actually had the advantage of living in a state that provided these early childhood services even before there was a federal program. These included regular home visits from a physical therapist who stretched his legs and helped him with his coordination, and from an occupational therapist who helped him put together a book of pictures he could point at to tell people what he wanted.

The Waupun School District in which Jon lived serviced a number of area communities, and during his early childhood he attended three different schools before going on to middle school and high school: preschool in Oakfield, kindergarten and first grade in Waupun, second grade in Mayville, and back to Waupun for third to fifth grade. It was in preschool that he began seeing a speech pathologist on a regular basis to work on his communication. His first speech pathologist, Mary Oja, had an office that consisted of a little cubicle in the corner of the school library that barely had enough room for Jon's wheelchair. Mary was the one who introduced him to his first word board, a tri-fold chart with about 200 words that had its own symbol system called "Bliss symbols" that he pointed to in order to communicate. Invented by Charles Bliss in the 1940s, and first used by Shirley McNaughton to teach children with CP in the early 1970s, the system that is now known as Blissymbolics utilizes about 4,500 authorized symbols, or Blisswords, which can be combined and recombined in countless ways to create new Blisswords. Blisswords, in turn, can be grammatically sequenced to form an expanding array of sentences (Bliss 1978; Blissymbolics Communication International n.d.). While this word board was a far cry from the computerized speech-generating device Jon uses today, it opened the world of communication to him, and learning how to communicate with his word board was as natural for him as it is for any child learning to speak. "But when I got angry," Jon admits, "or when someone else got angry at me, my communication would break down, which only escalated my volatile emotions."

During this time Jon also tried to express himself verbally, but only his family could understand the mumbled sounds he made. If he tried to talk to an outsider, someone in his family would have to translate what he was saying. This relates to something Jon has observed through his experiences with the AVA summer camp he started in 2001.

> Some of the kids are not motivated to learn how to use their device because they can get by in their families without it. Families may also be concerned that early use of augmentative communication may result in a decline in natural speech abilities of children, even though current research does not find this to be the case.[5] Still, if a person with a speech impairment stops trying to verbalize, it may become more difficult for family members to understand them. My sister Janeen tells me that she now has more trouble understanding me than she did before I acquired a state-of-the-art device, but that may simply be because we do not spend as much time together as we did when we were younger.

In school Jon also continued to receive physical therapy, a part of his therapeutic regimen that he hated, which was frustrating for the therapists who had to work with him. But Jon also was (is) a very competitive person. When his therapist would tell him that his friend Suzie had done so many sit-ups or rode so many miles on the exercise bicycle, he always wanted to beat her. "Overall," Jon admits, "the physical therapy helped a great deal with my mobility when I was out of my wheelchair, which mainly consisted of crawling, as well as my ability to independently transfer in and out of my chair."

Outside of not being able to speak, Jon thinks he experienced his childhood "as normally as any able-bodied kid." Janeen and him fought like cats and dogs, just like other siblings. He remembers having arguments over what they were going to watch on television, with Janeen feeling a little resentful that their mother would usually let Jon have his way. But mostly they have many fond memories of playing with each other.

> We played restaurant and built a fort out of an old army blanket that we slung over the railing of a loft we had in our house. We played with matchbox cars and with Play-Doh and finger paint when we were allowed to, because we would make quite a mess. We liked to throw all of the chair and sofa cushions on the floor, diving on top of them and crawling through the wedges between them. We played dress up and I particularly remember Janeen stuffing me into a Raggedy Ann Doll dress, tying strings in my hair. When we got a little older, our family would often go to Fond du Lac on Sundays to shop at the mall and grocery store. Often Janeen and I would stay in the car so mom and dad could finish their shopping more quickly. I remember playing the "made you look" game, listening to the radio together, and just talking.

Jeff, on the other hand, was generally out of the picture as far as Jon was concerned. He was 10 years older and off doing his own thing. What Jeff remembers most about those early years was the incessant crying, which he viewed as Jon's way of communicating and getting attention, and also as an outlet for his emotions. But Jeff, as well as Janeen, was not above trying to taunt Jon or make fun of him.

> Jeff likes to remind me of the time I woke up crying to the radio playing "You Light Up My Life." After that incident, he and Janeen would try to *make me cry* by singing the song to me. There was the time, too, when they found me on the floor bawling. They thought I had hurt myself only to find I had pulled a tag off the couch that said "do not remove under penalty of law." I was only about five years old at the time, but I could read the tag and thought I was going to jail. We can all laugh about it now, but I didn't find it so funny at the time. Maybe poking fun at me was their way of getting back at me for tattling to my parents if they did something wrong. My mom always knew that I could be counted on to blow the whistle on them.

Like Jon and his mother, as Jon and Jeff got older they could lock horns at times, which Jon thinks is because they are so much alike.

> Jeff and I are both stubborn and hard-headed, willing to do whatever it takes to achieve our goals. Growing up, I often felt that Jeff lacked confidence in my abilities, but now I realize he was only being the overprotective older brother. I remember that he didn't want me to start school because he was afraid the kids would pick on me because of my disability. And when he got his driver's license, and I was driving in the car with him, he would constantly ask me if I was okay.

Insofar as Janeen was closer to Jon's age, she had more of the responsibility to take care of him than Jeff and most other siblings with younger brothers or sisters who don't have disabilities.[6] During her teenage years she took care of Jon during the summers while Janet went to the meat market to help Al with the paperwork. Jon needed to be fed and Janeen did not like this job, in part because Jon was a messy eater.

> I'm prone to coughing when I eat, and Janeen would end up wearing my meal. One time she poured maple syrup on my head to get back at me. She first tried combing it out, but the comb kept getting stuck. So she had to wash my hair before our mom got home. Because I preferred our mom to feed me, we'd sometimes wait until five minutes before she came home to get everything ready, and when mom walked into the door Janeen would say, "Oh, I was just getting ready to feed Jon." I think mom was onto us, but she would feed me anyway.
>
> I think this is important for people to understand. Like many other people with disabilities, I saw myself as a normal kid and today see myself as a

normal guy. It's not that my disability is irrelevant to my life. How could it be? But my disability does not define me. [7] The problem, of course, is anticipated by the age-old adage: You can't judge a book by its cover. It's other people who define me in terms of my disability and all too often they don't take the time to get to know who Jon Feucht really is. This is an especially challenging dilemma because it takes me a longer time to communicate my thoughts than it does for verbally talking people.

Jon's early years in school also had a somewhat paradoxical impact on the way in which his disability shaped his self-identity. In kindergarten he was segregated in a special room with five other students with disabilities where they were instructed by one special education teacher, Mr. Max, and his classroom aide, Ann Hedman. On the one hand, Jon's time spent with these peers made him think that he was as normal as everyone else. On the other hand, his separation from the rest of the students made him feel different from everyone else.

As Jon looks back on those years, he thinks the segregated approach to his early childhood education may have been in violation of the EAHCA, which mandated that students with disabilities be educated in the "least restrictive environment." [8] At that time, however, exactly what constituted a "least restrictive environment" was subject to dispute, and it took a series of lawsuits and appellate court decisions between 1979 and 1994 to require schools to provide any supplemental aids, including assistive technology and teacher's aides, that were needed to integrate children in regular classrooms (Fleischer and Zames 2001).

> When I started school, I think that four or five of us, if not all six of us, could have been mainstreamed in a regular classroom if we had a teacher's aide to work with. Nevertheless, I am grateful to Ann, who worked so hard for me as a teacher's aide, who discovered my above-average abilities in mathematics, the first recognition by a school official that my CP and inability to speak had nothing to do with my intelligence.

By the time Jon entered first grade, there were only two other disabled students besides him who had remained in the school, and because this number was easier to manage, they were placed in a regular classroom with the assistance of a teacher's aide. Again this experience had a somewhat paradoxical impact on Jon. Because he was now being educated with nondisabled students, it helped him feel like everyone else. At the same time, his mainstream teacher did not want him in her class, and she even resisted meeting with Jon's mother at parent-teacher conferences. Jon thinks that "part of what she didn't like is the time it took for her to read what I was pointing to on my word board. But I also don't think she thought I was smart, and I obviously didn't get any encouragement for my academics from her."

In ways like this, therefore, Jon struggled with other's low expectations of his capabilities. And it was actually Jon's physical therapist, Audrey Rodar, not his teachers, who first told his parents that he was "college material." This came as a shock to them, because even they could not understand how a person with Jon's physical needs could go to college. Even later, when Jon decided to attend college, they still did not think he could do it. [9]

First grade was also noteworthy for being the time when Jon got his first power wheelchair. Because it was difficult to transport back and forth from his home to school, Jon kept the chair at school. The school bus would bring him to school in his manual chair, and then he would transfer into his power chair for the rest of the school day.

> I remember the first couple times I got into it I turned the speed up all the way and took off like a bat out of hell, crashing into furniture and whatever obstacles were in my way. Everyone shouted at me to slow down, and one time I got pinched at school for speeding in the hallway. Eventually my physical therapist worked with me to learn how to handle it more appropriately, but to this very day I'm prone to drive my chair fast. In Whitewater I can be seen motoring around town as fast as the sidewalk traffic will bear. I guess I have a need for speed. Even before I got my power wheelchair my friends would push me in my manual chair, pretending it was a race car and pushing me so fast that my front wheels would start to shake and rattle uncontrollably. One time we hit a big crack in the parking lot and the chair tipped over forward and I landed full force on my face. I had taken falls before, but never one like this. I got two black eyes, scratching up my face pretty badly and barely missing a broken nose.

It was in the second grade that Jon's parents bought him a rudimentary speech-generating device, which produced a robot-like sound that was difficult for people to understand. Jon remembers the exact date, January 28, 1986, because it was the day of the *Challenger* space shuttle explosion. He recalls spending a very long time at an assistive technology center trying out different devices before selecting this one, which the salesman said would be obsolete even before he got home.

> In some ways I don't actually consider this my first device because I never felt comfortable using it. It took me a long time to input what I wanted to say because I had to type everything out letter by letter. Since the voice was virtually unintelligible, the person I was talking to had to look over my shoulder to view the message on a little screen that wasn't much bigger than a calculator. On the other hand, it did have a cool feature that allowed me to print out words on an adding machine-sized slip of paper, which came in handy for spelling tests at school.

For the most part Jon continued to use his word board as his main form of communication, and his experience with his first computerized device is not uncommon. Research on the use of speech-generating technology by people with disabilities finds that it is common for such devices to be abandoned early—because they may be difficult to use or fail to deliver the hoped-for results.[10] They are also rather expensive, and there is little technical support for the assistance that is needed to set up and maintain the equipment. Even speech pathologists are often unfamiliar with these devices. Nowadays Jon likes to tell this joke: "Five hundred speech pathologists walk into a bar and order one beer. The bartender is puzzled, and asks, 'One beer?' One of the speech pathologists answers, 'Yes, one beer, for the one who knows how to use an AAC device.'"

By the time Jon got to the second grade at Parkview Elementary School in nearby Mayville, he was beginning to feel a sense of impermanency with the teacher's aides, physical therapists, and speech pathologists he had been working with. He would get attached to them, only to have them leave or not follow him to the next school. Jon also became aware that he worked better with some people than others. Over the years he found that some of these professionals seem to think that all they need in order to do their job effectively is apply the technical training they have learned in school, not realizing or caring that an equally important part of their job is developing a personal rapport with the children they work with. In Jon's lifetime he has worked with professionals of both stripes.

Two of the physical therapists whom Jon had the good fortune of working with over an extended period of time were Ellen Decker (for 10 years) and Amy Yudes (for 5 years). When he first met Ellen and Amy, Jon was purposefully naughty with them, testing them to see if they would stay even if he was a brat.

> I kicked them when they tried to tie my shoes and wouldn't listen to them when they'd tell me to do something. I would do anything but lie, because I was taught to always tell the truth. But they put up with me, knowing what I was doing, and we developed a powerful chemistry with each other. I remember that I talked with Ellen for hours about God and the spiritual side of life, and with Amy about nature, hunting, and fishing—today I am a devout Christian and fishing is my favorite pastime.

Parkview also was an important experience for Jon because they did everything and anything they could to make him feel like any other student. Whenever they went on a field trip, he was included. He remembers the time his mother went along as a chaperone on a trip to the capitol building in Madison. The supervising teacher designated Janet as the tour guide for Jon and three or four of his classmates. Jon thinks that this "teacher was surely not the brightest person for giving my mom this assignment, because she got our group lost."

During this period of Jon's life he also developed many friendships that made him feel like an ordinary kid. Andy and he both loved baseball, and they talked about it all the time. Like many other kids who love sports, Jon remembers dreaming about becoming a Major League pitcher, an unrealistically absurd fantasy, he realized, for a kid with CP. But, then again, such fantasies are just as unrealistic for most able-bodied kids who dream of becoming professional athletes. In this respect Jon was no different from most other kids.

Jason was another one of Jon's good friends. He met him in the third grade and did not really like him at first. But by the time they got into the fourth grade, they were inseparable. Jason and his two brothers would come over to Jon's house almost every Saturday to hang out. They wrestled on the bed and played basketball on their knees with a lowered hoop. Jon recalls, "It was great to have a friend like that!"

Jon thinks that he benefited a lot from the fact that his parents never babied him. They encouraged him to play in the dirt, jump into piles of leaves, and swing in their tire swing. Before he started crawling, around two years of age, he would scoot himself on his back with his legs, but once he started to crawl, he could get around fairly well. He remembers the time he crawled across two yards to visit his neighbors Bill and Jane. "They were surprised to see me," he recalls, "and wondered why my mother would let me do that."

Jon also had a rebellious streak that he thinks was associated with his stubbornness. He remembers a time when he was horsing around with his classmates in music class. When the teacher, Mrs. Fuller, told them to stop, he didn't—he was somewhat of the class clown—and she sent him to the corner for a punitive time-out. When Jon got over to the corner, he turned around and flipped her off.

I was only seven years old and all I knew was that it meant something bad. But this type of obstinacy that I exhibited at an early age was also part of my drive. I was always one to work and work until I accomplished what I set out to do. Setting goals and achieving them has always been my drug of choice. Sometimes the idea of becoming successful has taken over my life. I think this may have been a way for me to compensate for my disability, or perhaps because I'm a perfectionist, or maybe I have a fear of failure. The downside of all this was that I was always an anxious person—hence my one-time generalized anxiety disorder diagnosis. I even worried about passing kindergarten, if you can imagine that.

When Jon was ready for middle school, which started in the sixth grade, he was faced with a school in Waupun that was housed in a multiple-story building that had no elevator. Since this school was out of the question, his parents lobbied to have him enrolled in the school in nearby Brandon, which was more accessible.

> I was devastated that I couldn't go to middle school with my friends, and the students in Brandon were not particularly welcoming. This was partly due to the fact that they thought I was given special treatment by the teachers. When I entered the new school, the teachers told the students to treat me like every-body else. But gradually they saw that I didn't get into trouble for doing the things that got other students into trouble. I remember the time I forgot to bring my spelling book to school, the consequence for which was supposed to be after-school detention. That also was the day my dad was going to take me to the Milwaukee Brewers baseball game later that evening. I knew that if I got a detention my dad wouldn't take me to the game that night, or worse, he'd take me to the game and be mad at me the whole time. I begged and begged and made a big scene about not getting a detention. The teacher gave into me and this really annoyed my classmates.

During this period of Jon's life he was also the recipient of a lot of teasing, which was more than your friendly kind of childhood bantering—it was meant to humiliate him. He particularly remembers one boy who sat next to him and continually chanted "retard, retard" loud enough so that everyone else could hear. But the worst of it came from a bully named Kyle, who made Jon's life a living nightmare.

> Kyle was downright mean, and he knew how to get under my skin to get me to blow up and get myself in trouble. Every time I responded in kind by swearing in my mumbled voice or flipping him off, he'd tell the teachers on me. We'd be sent to the principal's office and our parents would be asked to come in. But only Kyle's parents came to defend him. My parents thought I should learn to fight my own battles, and this had the effect of forcing me to advocate for myself, a lesson I learned well.

While attending middle school, Jon had an influential social studies teacher, Mr. Cates, who intrigued him with his knowledge of history and collection of historical memorabilia that he brought to class—army helmets, cannonballs, rocket launchers and the like. One thing Mr. Cates always stressed was the importance of getting a good education so the students wouldn't end up becoming burger flippers at the local McDonald's. "The first time he said this really made me think," Jon recalls. "I knew I couldn't do manual work, and that I needed to go to college. So I spent my middle and high school years focusing on academics and getting good grades, which wasn't much of a sacrifice since I didn't have too much of a social life."

Jon realized that he was a pretty bright youth—he made the honor roll every semester—and he seemed to catch on to things a little faster than most students. He had a good memory and a facility with numbers. But he has also struggled with reading, probably an undiagnosed learning disability that may be associated with his CP.

> My reading comprehension has been good enough to get by, but I do much better when the material is converted to audio output. I can read and comprehend each and every word, but my eyes have trouble moving through an entire paragraph. I may have some type of reading-related learning disability, but all my life I've been afraid to get tested. With all my physical challenges, I always felt that my mind was my biggest asset, and I just couldn't entertain the idea that I might have a cognitive disability too.

In August of 1992 Jon was ready to start high school, excited to return to Waupun, which had a high school that was accessible, and become reacquainted with his old friends. It made him feel good about himself when some of them told him they were glad to see him again. By now he had become somewhat of a local celebrity. During summers he would ride along when his father made deliveries, and he got to meet a lot of people in the community. "I developed a reputation as this significantly disabled kid of parents who owned a popular meat market who was bright and cocky, who liked to joke and trash talk and who could take a joke himself."

In high school Jon still struggled with other people's doubts about whether he could actually go to college, doubts he was determined to resist but which also seeped into his thinking. One setback was a record-keeping class he took during his freshman year. The teacher, who seemed past the age of retirement, had no rapport with the students. She assigned a lot of homework involving spreadsheets that Jon's teacher's aide had to set up so he could enter the data himself, and he had difficulty keeping up. It was at this time that he started thinking that he needed to tone down his expectations and enroll in a two-year technical college rather than a four-year university.

During this time in Jon's life he also started to experience bouts of dramatic mood swings. He would vacillate from being a bold and cocky guy, until he said something that got him into trouble, upon which he would become more introverted and go into a state of depression for weeks on end until he snapped out of it.

> I had weeks when I was higher than a kite that were followed by awful crashes. The littlest thing would set me off, even a wrong word, and I'd get worked up to the point that I'd start sweating profusely and acting like an animal. I started fighting more with my parents, which put a lot of stress on our home life, and then stew over it and feel bad about myself for months. I now understand this behavior to be a consequence of a bipolar disorder, but no one realized this at the time. I don't know if hormones or stress brought this on, but it was a chemical imbalance that wasn't treated properly until I was in my thirties.

At this time there were few people who Jon could truly trust. One of them was his best friend BJ. Jon remembers a homecoming election during his sophomore year when all the students decided to vote the "dorks" onto the homecoming court.

> BJ got mad when I asked him if he was going to vote for me. BJ said there was no way he would do that. But outside of him, I always felt that even if people were nice to me they probably were laughing at me behind my back. If it wasn't for BJ and two study hall teachers who were sources of emotional support, I don't think I would have made it through high school.
>
> One of these teachers, Steve Lenz, taught social studies and was a younger man who had grown up in Waupun. I thought it was cool that he knew my sister and parents. We established a great rapport, and I felt I could talk to him about anything or simply shoot the breeze. If I had problems with other kids picking on me or an argument at home, he was the first one I'd talk to about it. He never made a big deal about my disability and was always patient listening to what I had to say.
>
> The other teacher, Chuck Stangl, was the teacher who was assigned to the students with emotional difficulties. I'll always remember the first time I saw him he had had a mullet and was wearing a white dress shirt with a matching flowery tie and suspenders. He had an aura about him and I knew right away that we'd get along wonderfully; he became like a second father to me. We'd play cards, joke with each other, try to stump each other with sports trivia questions, and most importantly, follow the Green Bay Packers together. I think it was sometime in my junior year that I was put into his eighth hour study hall and we both knew we wouldn't get any work done. We became life-long friends, and after I graduated high school we'd meet online and play cribbage and just talk for hours about life.

Having Mr. Lenz and Mr. Stangl to talk to helped Jon a lot, and combined with his rebellious nature, he eventually regained his focus and never lost sight of his desire to obtain his slice of the American dream. Even though he had doubts as to whether he could succeed in college, he never let on to this because he did not want to give anybody, his parents especially, a reason to stop him. "Whatever I've had going against me," he says, "one of my strongest attributes is that I have an innate ability to envision the future and map out a strategy to get where I want to be. I was determined to not be the guy with a disability who graduates high school, collects disability insurance, and disappears into the woodwork never to be heard from again."

During the summer following Jon's junior year, he attended a wheelchair sports camp for youths with disabilities at the University of Wisconsin-Whitewater, a physically accessible campus that has an official mission within the University of Wisconsin System to serve students with disabilities. UWW was just a little over an hour's drive from Jon's home, and he had heard about the school from friends of his parents who had children who had gone there. At the camp, Jon couldn't do everything the other kids who used push wheelchairs and had less significant disabilities could do, but the camp coordinator Mike Frogley found ways to adapt each sport for him. When they played basketball, Mike told Jon to position his chair on the edge of the paint at the defensive end and get in the way of any opposing player who tried to get by him. One time when a player tried to get off a shot, Jon raised and flexed his arms and blocked it! "Mike and I really got a kick out of that," Jon recalls. "After that camp, I knew where I wanted to go to college."

NOTES

1. The life history tradition as sociological method can be traced to the work of W. I. Thomas and Florian Znaniecki (1918–20) and the classic period of Chicago school sociology (Berger 2008a; Luken and Vaughan 1999). The general distinction between life history and life story is that the latter makes greater use of an informant's first-person account (Atkinson 1998; Denzin 1989; Plummer 2001).

2. Scholarly inquiry about storytelling, often referred to as narrative inquiry, is a thriving interdisciplinary endeavor (Berger and Quinney 2005; Bochner 2001; Clandinin 2013; Polletta et al. 2011; Taylor 2001).

3. For sociological work that more narrowly construes the American dream in terms of financial success, see Merton (1938) and Messner and Rosenfeld (2001).

4. For sources on the nature, etiology, diagnosis, and treatment of bipolar disorder, see Joseph and Jamison (2007); National Institute of Mental Health (2008); Yatham (2010). For memoirs, see Bergen (1999); Jamison (1995).

5. See Clark et al. (2001); Harris (2010); Hodge (2007); Jacobs et al. (2004); Lasker and Bedrosian (2001); Millar, Light, and Schlosser (2006).

6. Research on the nature of the relationship between disabled and nondisabled siblings has yielded mixed results. Some studies have found that nondisabled siblings feel resentful for having to put their lives "on hold" while the family gathers its resources to take care of a disabled child. Some nondisabled siblings feel embarrassment, guilt, or concern about their disabled sibling's future. But others learn to become more caring, compassionate individuals. Like Janeen, they often need to help out more with caretaking than would otherwise be the case if their sibling was not disabled (Grossman 1972; Marshak, Seligman, and Prezant 1999; Meyer 1995; Naseef 2001; Solomon 2012).

7. See Engel and Munger (2003); Juette and Berger (2008); Watson (2002).

8. For literature on the controversies surrounding contemporary special education services and the policy of inclusion vs. exclusion in mainstream classrooms, see Barton and Armstrong (2001); Connor and Ferri (2007); Danforth (2009); Lipsky and Gartner (1997). Margret Winzer and Kaz Mazurek describe the general state of U.S. classrooms at the dawn of the twenty-first century this way: "Although the most significant movement toward general classrooms has occurred in the disabilities categories that include students with the milder disabilities—learning disabilities, speech and language impairments, orthopedic impairments, and other health problems—in all other categories there is a trend toward moving students into less restrictive settings" (2000:xii).

9. Janet and Al's reactions are indicative of what Andrew Solomon (2012) characterizes as *vertical* and *horizontal* identities. According to Solomon, vertical identities entail intrafamilial traits that are passed on from one generation to the next, with most children sharing at least some traits with their parents. Horizontal identities, on the other hand, entail traits that are foreign to parents and therefore require children to acquire identity through extrafamilial experiences.

10. See note 5.

Chapter Three

Finding a Voice

As stages in the life course, adolescence and adulthood are best conceptualized as social constructions, not definitive statuses, and the transition between them can be murky (Eisenstadt 1956). Once a person reaches legal adulthood—in the United States typically at 18 years of age—the prolonged years of post-high school schooling that many undertake often keeps them in a dependent status vis-à-vis their parents. Nowadays the complete transition to adulthood takes longer than in the past, extending well into people's twenties. Sue Caton and Carolyn Kagan (2007) argue that it becomes increasingly difficult to identify a "normal" sequence of life course events that people go through. Many people in their twenties, for example, move in and out of their parents' homes after first leaving, experience a period of employment before going to college, both work and attend college at the same time, have children without being married, and raise children while going to school.

It is in this context that the particular challenges facing people with disabilities transitioning to adulthood needs to be considered. To begin with, only 65 percent of youths with serious disabilities even graduate from high school, to say nothing of going on to college, compared to 79 percent of youths with mild disabilities and 89 percent of youths without disabilities (Hogan 2012). All too often, high school youths with disabilities receive little assistance from high school counselors. In a study of the high school transition experience, Valerie Leiter (2012) found that disabled youths were especially critical of the lack of help they received from high school guidance counselors, with less than 25 percent of students even talking with their counselors in the year prior to graduation. At the same time, for those going on to college, some of the accommodations and special education services they received during high school may no longer be available, and the facilities of the institution may not be physically accessible.

This is not the case at the University of Wisconsin-Whitewater, a completely accessible campus that has been serving students with disabilities as part of its special mission within the University of Wisconsin System since the 1970s. And while Jon was in high school, he had the good fortune of meeting Connie Wiersma, director of instructional technology for Disabled Student Services at UWW, who came to his school as part of an outreach grant she had received from the Division of Vocational Rehabilitation to help with students transitioning from high school to college. Connie would become one of Jon's mentors and one of his closest friends, the person who introduced him to the computerized speaking device that would change his life.

At the time, Jon's parents did not want him to go to college, thinking he could not make it on his own. And whenever he would subsequently falter, he would be ridden with self-doubt and think that maybe they were right. But Jon was stubborn and determined to prove them wrong. Today he tells young people with significant disabilities that they should always respect their parents, but that does not mean they should always take their advice. [1] They may be the only disabled person their parents know, and their parents may be unaware of the opportunities that are available for them.

When Jon first met Connie he was still relying on a word board to communicate, and when he arrived at Whitewater it proved inadequate. There was one incident during his first year at college that was a turning point in this regard. As Jon recalls:

> I rolled up to the information desk in the university center to ask the student worker a question, about what I no longer remember. I started pointing to my word board and she didn't understand. I got frustrated and started flailing my arms and making guttural sounds, scaring her so much that she called the police. I high-tailed it out of there, but that's when I knew I needed something more.

Shortly thereafter, Connie stopped Jon in the hallway by DSS and said, "Perfect, you're here, follow me." They went into a conference room and met with three other students and a representative of the Prentke Romich Company to try out what was at that time a state-of-the art Liberator speech-generating device. It used a software language code called Minispeak (called Unity today), and to use it proficiently you had to know your parts of speech. Some of the other students with speech impairments that Connie was working with had trouble using it, but Jon was her success case. Jon remembers how excited his parents were when he first called them and said, *"This is your son Jon."*

Getting the Liberator device changed Jon's life, and being a person of religious faith—he was raised in the Catholic Church and considers himself to be a born-again Christian—he looks back on that day as part of a larger plan God had for him. But in the short term, Jon still had to learn there was more to the art of communication than speaking—like how to initiate and end a conversation. Jon was used to very short, abrupt conversational exchanges—get to the point and that's it. One time he said what he had to say to Connie and started to leave. She said, "Jon! I have something to say yet. Don't go away. I'm not finished." Jon would be so absorbed in typing into his device that he would neglect to make eye contact with the person he was speaking to and read the expression on their face.

Then, of course, there was the other side of the coin: the person with whom he is speaking has to be patient and wait for him to complete his thoughts. Not everyone is willing to do this. Because of the sordid history of societal treatment of people with disabilities, they are still often viewed and responded to by nondisabled people in terms of a negative social type—as physical or cognitive deviants—that attributes common symbolic meaning to disparate individuals. In sociologist Erving Goffman's terms, the stigma associated with disability is constituted by a "spoiled identity" whereby the person is "reduced in our minds from a whole and usual person to a tainted, discounted one" (1963:3). Anthropologist Robert Murphy adds that all too many nondisabled people view people with disabilities as a "fearsome possibility," displacing their fears that "it could happen to them" onto the disabled person (1987:117).

One experience that Jon had in a physical geography class taught by Professor David Travis is illustrative.[2] Most of the students who were enrolled in the class were there to fulfill a general science elective requirement. The class consisted of four lectures and one lab per week. The classroom was rather small and filled to capacity, with the students packed closely together and enough space to fit a wheelchair or two. Jon could tell that the other students were uncomfortable with him, trying to get as far away as possible.

Early on in the course Jon did not talk in class, but would speak to Professor Travis after class to ask questions. In this way, Travis began familiarizing himself with Jon's manner of speech, learning to be patient as Jon completed his remarks. Jon also saw Travis in his office to set up the accommodations he needed through DSS, which included an in-class note-taker and provisions for taking examinations. It was during these exchanges that Jon and Travis began to develop a rapport.

A turning point in the class, and Jon's relationship with the other students, occurred during a story Travis was telling about chasing a tornado, one of his professional interests and personal avocations. Travis was driving with his infant daughter asleep in a car-seat in the rear, when a tornado warning came on the weather radio he kept in his vehicle. His wife was at work, and he thought about taking his daughter to her office before proceeding with his chase. But he did not want to wake her, so he decided to follow the tornado *with his daughter in the car!*

As Travis was telling this story, Jon was frantically waving his arms. "Do you have a question?" Travis asked. Jon had a big grin on his face, and the entire class waited to hear what he had to say as he finished typing and then played his remarks: "I really feel sorry for your wife. How has she not left you by now?" With that, everyone in the class broke out in laughter. And it was at that moment that the other students finally recognized Jon's humanity, that he was attuned to everything Travis was saying and that he had the same reaction to the story as they did. Indeed, many of the other students had been shaking their heads in disbelief as if to say, "Are you kidding?" "What kind of father are you?" What Jon had inadvertently accomplished was what other ethnographies of social interaction have revealed: that people with disabilities are sometimes able to ward the imposition of a spoiled identity through impression management strategies such as refusing assistance to demonstrate competency or using humor to make others feel comfortable (Cahill and Eggleston 1994, 1995; see also Berger 2012b).

As the semester went on, Jon became more verbal in class, offering his opinion on all sorts of topics, from global warming to overpopulation. When Travis posed a question to the students, Jon was the first to raise his hand. As a result, the other students began seeing that he was pretty smart. And as he continued to crack jokes, they began to feel more comfortable with him. Jon always had a pretty good sense of humor, and now that he could talk, he was coming into his own as a comedian.

Prior to the tornado story incident, none of the other students had wanted to work with Jon in the lab. Travis had asked the students to select a lab partner and work in pairs, but Jon was working on his own with his student aide who wrote down the results of his work. But after the tornado story, some of the other students started coming over to Jon to ask *him* questions about the lab work and how he got the answer to a particular assignment. In turn, some of them would help Jon with some of the fine-motor-skill work required to manipulate the lab instruments. It was as if they had completely forgotten what it was that had made them uncomfortable with Jon in the first place.

It is a fact of life that most people are uncomfortable with people who are different, and psychologists Nancy Miller and Catherine Sammons (1999) identify three general types of differences that provoke varied responses from others: *Unfamiliar differences* are those that are new to the observer, *unexpected differences* are those that are familiar but in a different context, and *unsettling differences* are those that are disturbing. In Jon's case, the students in Travis's class were likely to have seen someone with his level of disability before, but not necessarily in a close-knit classroom for four days a week. At the same time, it is also likely that these students had never encountered an articulate individual who uses a computerized communication device, and once exposed to someone like Jon, the differences that at first seemed unsettling began to seem more benign. Be that as it may, it is also true that Jon is someone who demands to be noticed. He is not the type of person who wants to blend into the background and pretend that he, and his disability differences, don't exist. As Jon says, "I want to be someone whom others take into account."

College is not all about academics, of course, especially for someone who needs assisted care and where meeting your daily needs of living can be a struggle. And Jon, like others with significant disabilities who have tried to live on their own, has had many problems with paid care workers over the years (Meyer, Donelly, and Weerakoon 2007). Take a woman named Ella, for example, whose life history is reported in a study by Nikki Wedgwood (2011). Ella was born without limbs, except for a portion of one of her legs, and she is dependent on assistive care for her independence. But during college she had problems with care workers not showing up or not looking after her properly, such as only taking her to the toilet three times a day, which caused her to develop a urinary tract infection. To remedy this problem, Ella found a new care agency, but even then problems persisted. In fact, Ella was only able to continue in college because her brother Dan was attending the school at the same time, living in the room directly above hers. Ella says that when her care workers "didn't show up in the mornings to get [her] out of bed," Dan would have to help her (p. 444). "He's taken me in emergencies when I've had to go to the toilet and stuff. . . . If the lift isn't working he lifts me and that sort of thing." Ella says she used to be more ambitious about what she wanted to accomplish in her life, priding herself on being a trailblazer for people with serious disabilities. But now she thinks, "Trailblazing sucks! It's not all it's cracked up to be!"

In Jon's experience, he has found that some care workers seem to think that it is Jon who works *for them*, rather than they who work *for him*, which Jon says makes him feel like a "zoo animal" and always nervous about not knowing what to expect when he gets a new assistant. Two male aides in particular stand out in Jon's mind.

> There was this one guy I had during my first year at Whitewater while I was living in the dorm who was an alcoholic. He didn't come to work drunk, but he seemed like his only thought was to look forward to getting off work so he could get his next drink. Another aide was an atheist who gave me a hard time about my religious beliefs and whose disrespect for my faith definitely rubbed me the wrong way. When I called the agency office to complain, they blew me off, telling me I had to work with the people they send me. When I got angry and started talking back to this care worker, he said, "Do you want me to turn

your fucking computer off?" When he said that, I got so mad that I punched him in the jaw.

Eventually the agency called my parents and told them that if I didn't cool down they couldn't continue with my services. My parents came down to Whitewater and took me home for the weekend. Maybe it was my bipolar kicking in or my depression; in either case, I felt suicidal. I knew I had to start accepting the fact that I wasn't always going to get my way or I'd ruin my future. When I got back to school, a friend was playing Garth Brooks's "The River." I can still hear the lyrics about the Lord helping Brooks through rough waters calling out to me. I started to cry and asked God to help me make it through college—and provide me with assisted care.

Around this time Jon also had a problem with a wheelchair salesman. Jon had ordered a new power wheelchair in November, and still had not gotten it by May.

I tried to be patient but the delay was ridiculous, and I finally sent him a fax saying it was "bullshit" that the chair hadn't come. That's all I said, but he proceeded to call my parents and lie to them that I had complained to his boss, and then threatened to cancel my order because he didn't want to have anything to do with me. I was frantic and in tears, and when one of my friends tried to get me to explain what was going on, I thought he was going to slap me in the face to calm me down.

To this day I think that the incompetency of this salesman was inexcusable, but it was another example of letting my emotions get the better of me. I have always lived my life by my own version of the Golden Rule—I apply it only to those people who treat me well. If you do something wrong to me, I will react strongly and lash out against you. I don't think there is anything wrong to want to hold people to account, but I think my overreaction in circumstances like these, my tendency to get in their face, was probably related to my bipolar condition. I also think my reaction comes from my fear that people are trying to sabotage my independence, to keep me cloistered at home or put me in a residential facility or group home.

College life is full of distractions from academics for many students, and this was true for Jon, too. There was a lot of drinking and partying in the dorms. During his first year of college, his parents came down every two or three weeks to clean his room and bring him plates of food (his mother was so worried about his food allergies that she thought he would starve). When his parents would visit, they'd be horrified at the booze bottles and beer kegs that were left over from the prior night's activities. Jon realized he had to get out of the dorm or his grades would suffer and he would get kicked out of school. He moved into an apartment complex that catered to people with disabilities, but this place was infested with even more drugs than the dorms. One time the police were called to his apartment and his father had to come down to vouch for him and convince them that Jon was not a criminal.

Lest the reader be mistaken, through all this Jon was still making progress toward his goal—graduation from college. In this respect, he was not unlike other college students who avert a downward spiral and manage to get their act together before it is too late. Jon remained a driven person and his dream of success was his "drug of choice."

Jon says he always had a knack for computers—hence his ready adaption to his computerized speaking device—and he started out as a computer science major. But he just didn't have the passion for it. Rather, he wanted to do something where he could help other young people like him. He talked to Connie and the assistant director of DSS, who Jon prefers to remain anonymous, about getting into a counseling program and becoming a counselor. Connie was supportive, but the assistant director was not, saying Jon was not suited for this line of work because he could not communicate like other people. Mind you, this was coming from someone who claimed to be an advocate for students with disabilities!—which was not Jon's only disappointment with DSS.

In any case, Jon ended up majoring in psychology with a minor in English writing and received his bachelor of science degree in 2003. It took him a little longer to get his degree than most students, but he did it nonetheless. Throughout all this he developed a system of studying that helped him through school. He would start every assignment within 24 hours of when it was given and keep at it until it was done. "I never procrastinated," he says, "even if it stressed me out. I can't remember which professor taught me to do that, but it was one of the most valuable lessons I ever learned."

While he was attending college, Jon started a consulting business on the side teaching people with disabilities how to use their communication devices. He called the business Authentic Voices of Wisconsin. The idea for the name came from a friend who had interviewed him for a paper she was writing for a special education class. The project was called Authentic Voices, and Jon was immediately drawn to the idea of authenticity. Out of necessity and personal inclination he had always been a very direct person, never holding back from telling people how he felt. Of course, as Jon realizes, "This style of communication can rub some people the wrong way, and some people see me as a hard ass because I don't let anyone or anything get in my way."

Then, in the summer of 1999, another friend was attending an AAC summer camp in Colorado. When he told Jon about the camp, Jon started thinking about organizing a similar camp at Whitewater. After all, there was already a disability sports camp, among numerous camp programs for non-disabled students in sports, music, and cheerleading. "Why not," he thought, "set up something for kids learning how to use and become more proficient at using AAC, with an eye toward helping them become productive members of society?"

Jon first broached the idea with Connie and Dr. Richard (Dick) Lee, Dean of the Graduate School. Dick had administrative jurisdiction over the office of Continuing Education (CE), which in turn, included all the summer camp programs. Dick set up a meeting with Connie and Lou Zahn, the director of CE, to discuss the idea. Everyone was on board with the concept, and Connie suggested calling it Starting the Dream. When they realized they couldn't have a camp with the acronym STD, Jon suggested Authentic Voices of Wisconsin. Lou pointed out that they needed a name that could attract people from outside of the state, so they decided upon Authentic Voices of America.

At first, Dick had been skeptical about the camp, mainly because he didn't think they could manage the complex nature of the disabilities the campers might have. But Jon convinced him it would be fine as long as the campers brought their own aides—either one or two of their parents or a paid caregiver. Then there was the question of money. How would they pay for room and board in the dorms for the campers and their attendants, as well as the insurance, instructional training by a speech pathologist, transportation and admission fees for field trips, camp T-shirts, administrative costs, and so forth? Dick and Lou thought they would need to charge about $1,400 for a five-day camp to make it doable. Even then they would need extra money to cover financial assistance for those who could not afford it, as well as unanticipated cost overruns. For several years Dick provided seed money from CE, without which the camp would have never gotten off the ground. Eventually they separated the camp financially from the university and established AVA as a nonprofit organization, raising money through an annual golf outing and other charitable contributions.

> One of the first things we did is put together a planning committee, with representatives from Continuing Education, DSS, and the UWW Department of Communicative Disorders; and Dick provided travel funds for some of us to attend other camps to see what they were doing. I had the opportunity to do a two-week internship at an AAC program at Temple University in Philadelphia during the summer of 2000, which was one of the most profound experiences of my life. I remember witnessing a girl tell her mother that she loved her—for the first time in her life! There are no words to describe the feeling I had at that moment, and it's what drives me to this day.
>
> It was a little scary in Philadelphia, because the university is in a poor part of town. I wasn't used to seeing homeless people all over the place begging for money. At first I thought it was a bad idea to have an AAC program in this part of the city. But then I thought that maybe it was a good thing, because it forced those in attendance, myself included, to learn how to negotiate a more challenging environment.
>
> Another thing that stands out in my mind from the Temple experience was the opportunity to meet a disability activist who was a little older than me. Karen's disability was more severe than mine, but she never let that stop her from doing what she wanted to do. Her style of changing the world is different

than mine, however. She believes in protesting, blocking access to inaccessible places, and things like that. She has been arrested for her efforts and is proud of her actions. I'm grateful for people like Karen, but that kind of activism is not for me. Frankly, I'm glad I wasn't born earlier when people with disabilities had to fight for everything they got. Without question, I've had to fight, too, but not like my predecessors. I see myself more like a social scientist and a teacher, wanting to make people's *minds* rather than *buildings* accessible. Without a doubt, if it wasn't for those like Karen who pushed for legal reforms like the Education for All Handicapped Children Act and the Americans with Disabilities Act, there wouldn't be a Jon Feucht who had a chance to achieve the American dream. There wouldn't be an AVA to help change the lives of young people who need AAC to have their shot at this dream, too.

In my opinion, it is noteworthy that we got more support for AVA from Dick's office than we did from DSS. Whereas Dick poured thousands of dollars into AVA, the longtime DSS director never had much interest in developing programs for students like me who have more significant disabilities. His pet project was the wheelchair basketball program, which had become one of the elite programs in the country, indeed the entire world.[3] Dick, on the other hand, was more broadly attuned to the entire range of students with disabilities. It's not that he didn't love the basketball players. Indeed, his office was in the same building as DSS and the practicing gym for the team. He liked to hang out with the players and shoot baskets and talk trash with them. But he treated me the same way. We loved to banter, and every time I'd get in a good verbal shot, he threatened to sue me for electronic abuse. Dick was the master of the joke, but he knew when to be serious. I'll always remember one thing in particular he said to me: "Jon, the measure of a man is what it takes to make him give up, and I know you haven't given up on anything." And with his encouragement, I set my sights on graduate school.

Jon thinks that one of the tragedies of his experience at UWW, a sentiment that Ron holds as well, was the university politics that forced Dick, one of our most beloved colleagues, to leave. The long-time director of DSS had tolerated a number of abuses. There were people in the office, for example, who came to work and ignored their responsibilities, working on other "moonlighting" jobs they had outside of the university. There were also staff members who helped some students with their exams, which they took at DSS under approved accommodations guidelines, to bolster the graduation success rate of the program.

When the director retired, Dick was put in charge of the program for a couple of years and tried to address the problems. One of the workers whose dereliction of responsibilities Dick tried to redress happened to be African American, and when Dick tried to get her to change, she lodged a complaint with the university's Human Resources Department. During an inquiry led by the affirmative action officer, Dick was accused of being a racist, reprimanded by the administration, and forced to leave. Upon his departure, his replacement asked Jon to separate AVA from Continuing Education and form it as an independent nonprofit organization.

Those of us who know the inside story about what happened to Dick felt that an injustice had been done. In the short run, Dick landed an even better job at the University of Nevada, Las Vegas, but he died suddenly in 2009 of physical problems he was having. Those of us who knew him were stunned and saddened by his too early death. As for DSS, now called the Center for Students with Disabilities, it has for the most part been cleaned up and is doing a better job of serving the needs of the students.

All told, Jon spent the better part of two years planning for the first AVA camp, which made its debut in the summer of 2001, deciding on a two-part format that he used for the first 11 years of the camp.[4] First, each day of the camp opened with a session called "Straight Talk." In this part Jon delivered a pre-recorded speech, pausing at periodic intervals to solicit group discussion, which covered a particular theme. Over the years some of these themes included: what it means to be disabled, the challenges and opportunities of using communication devices, how to work with attendants, how to be a self-advocate, overcoming fears, and what makes for a successful life (Feucht 2004). It is an empowering experience for young people to hear someone like Jon talk about experiences that are relevant to their lives. And Jon realizes that he is a role model for them, and yes, even an inspiration, who shows them that they, too, can accomplish what he has accomplished in his life.

The second component of the camp consisted of "Communicative Activities" led by a speech pathologist. The purpose of these sessions was to get the campers to communicate with each other. For the most part the youths attending AVA have never spoken with another person who uses a computerized device, especially someone of their own age. This, too, is an empowering experience. As Jon observes:

> It helps the kids understand that they are not alone, that others share their problems, their hopes and dreams. During these sessions the campers develop their communication skills and the confidence to use them. And it is truly special to see the bonds that form, even lifelong friendships, between the campers, especially after they return to AVA and become camp "veterans."

The first camp was like a coming out party for Jon. No one was sure how or if it would work out. Only six people signed up, and only five showed up, and Jon thinks he got as much out of it as they did.

> I remember getting into a deep conversation with one of the campers about heroes. He said the fact that an AAC user was running the camp was a big part of why he came. He told me that I was more of a hero than people who play sports for a living. Later I came to question this kind of accolade, because

putting another person on a pedestal only sets the admirer up for disappointment when the "hero" can't live up to that billing. Still, that camp was very emotional for me, perhaps the most poignant time of my life. I remember rolling into Miller Park on our outing to a Milwaukee Brewers baseball game. For some reason the majestic setting hit me and I was so overcome with emotion that I couldn't even drive my chair; I had to have one of the camp assistants help me to our seats.

The camp had been a group effort, but afterwards the local newspapers only wanted to interview me, giving me all the credit when, in fact, the credit deserved to be shared. This left me with an uneasy, even lonely, feeling. I did not start AVA to show people how great I was; I don't want to be treated like some kind of supercrip. I still had a lot of self-demons to slay. And over the years I've had to tone down my expectations about what some of the campers will be able to achieve. Not all or even most of them are capable of becoming high-end users, and this became a point of contention as the camp began attracting more and more participants, including people with cognitive disabilities.

Jon admits that initially he had envisioned AVA as focusing on youths who were as intellectually capable as he. He realizes that some people may look down on him for that, questioning his moral integrity, thinking he is dismissing people with cognitive disabilities. But, Jon says:

I have to be honest, that is how I felt at the time, however "politically incorrect" that may seem. I've spent my whole life fighting against people who thought I was cognitively disabled. I think I was trying to prove that people who are physically disabled are as capable as nondisabled people at succeeding in intellectually demanding endeavors. Regardless, I realized that for the camp to grow and become financially viable, we had to expand my initial vision to be more inclusive. And in retrospect I think this is a good thing.

Jon's feelings on this matter are arguably part of a broader phenomenon that represents a divide between people with physical disabilities and people with cognitive disabilities, two diverse constituencies that "may have little in common except the stigma society imposes on them" (Engel and Munger 2003:14). Melvin Juette, whose story precipitated Jon's interest in publishing a book of his own, expresses similar sentiments (see chapter 1). After becoming disabled by a gunshot injury during his adolescence, Melvin was forced to enroll in a segregated high school where the city of Chicago sent all of its disabled students. Melvin was put into classes with students who had significant cognitive disabilities, and he felt as if *he* was being treated as if he *also* was cognitively disabled (Juette and Berger 2008). In this way, both Melvin and Jon express an existential concern with proving their cognitive competency in the face of the spoiled identity that is attributed to them because of their physical disabilities. [5]

NOTES

1. See Chapter 2, note 9.
2. We first recounted this story in Berger, Travis, and Feucht (2012).
3. See Berger (2009) and Juette and Berger (2008).
4. Beginning in 2012, Jon started to take a reduced role in the instructional activities of the camp, especially as he became more involved in the doctoral program at East Tennessee University.
5. Bernadette Baker (2002) thinks that disabled people like Jon and Melvin may be subjectively colonized by a concern with proving their autonomy. But for a critique of the colonization metaphor, see Sherry (2010).

Chapter Four

Days of Gloom, Days of Joy

Earlier we wrote that in fashioning the elements of Jon's story we began thinking about the nature of its narrative trajectory or arc. We noted that Jon's *quest* included getting a college education, and at this point in his life, operating a successful augmentative-alternative communication (AAC) summer camp. And we said there were times, prior to his bipolar disorder diagnosis in his mid-thirties, when Jon experienced his life less as a quest and more as a life filled with *chaos*.

Some of the life events that propelled Jon into chaos occurred over a 10–year span, between the early 1990s and early 2000s, involved the deaths of several significant others. These emotional stresses, when correlated with Jon's bipolar condition, pushed him into periodic depression and even suicidal ideation.

Talking about these facets of Jon's life proved difficult for him. Once he breached the subject and we asked him for further elaboration in our interview sessions, he paused for more than his usual moment of thoughtful silence before he responded. At times it appeared that tears were swelling up in his eyes. These moments were reminiscent of Anna Neumann's observations about "the interplay of text and silence in the stories of human lives" (1997:92). With most storied accounts, she observes, there "comes a silence that cannot be converted into words or understanding that is fully shared." The experience that is being remembered lives "in the gaze that comes with inward thought and inward talk." In Jon's case, the deaths that he continues to mourn were of people who had recognized his humanity, who had made him feel good about himself, who had helped him get beyond the moments of doubt brought on by others who dismissed him as inferior, as less than fully human.

Initially these moments of absence in Jon's story resembled what D. Jean Clandinin refers to as the "white spaces" of a text, "gaps that are left when stories intentionally or unintentionally are not told" (2013:209). With some probing, however, Jon offered brief accounts of these significant others, accounts that nonetheless may fail to convey the depth of the emotions he felt.

The first of these moments was the death of Ed, one of Jon's best friends, who Jon previously had left out of his story. "It was drugs," Jon laments, "that eventually did Ed in."

> To me, Ed was a good-hearted juvenile delinquent, a guy with earrings and tattoos, who smoked cigarettes and was always in trouble. But I'll always remember him as a gentle person who was kind to me and other people with disabilities. When he was graduating from high school, I talked to him about needing to stay as far away from drugs as possible. I've played that conversation back over and over in my mind. I wish Ed had listened.

Two years later, Jon's Uncle Charlie died of cancer. Jon thinks it was a military-related illness, because everyone in Charlie's army unit was dying of one kind of cancer or another. Charlie was a jokester, and even when he was weak and his body was wracked with cancer, he continued to make Jon laugh. Just a few months after that, Jon's Uncle Roger died, also of cancer. Jon remembers Roger as a man "who loved the outdoors, God and country, someone cast in my own image." In 1996 Jon's high school reading teacher Mrs. Steinbach died of cancer too. "She had a passion for learning that she imparted to me." That same year Chris, a dear friend who like Jon was disabled, died suddenly, the causes of which he is still unsure. "Chris was a role model for me, someone who always had a job while he was going to school, was always surrounded by friends, and never had a weekend that he spent alone. Chris was everything I wanted to be, though I didn't realize it until he was gone." In 1998 Joan, a family friend, died of a heart attack. "Our families went camping together a lot, and I have fond memories of playing cards and cribbage and just sitting around the campfire." In 2000 Sherry, another friend, died of cancer. Jon had met Sherry through a communication technology company she worked for. He had helped her with an AAC conference and they had become good friends. Jon says that "these are all people who helped make me the person I am today. They treated me with dignity, as just another guy, never patronizing me or seeing me through the lens of disability."

Most importantly, however, there was the death of Jon's grandfather in February 2002. It is somewhat ironic that Jon had not mentioned him until later in our interviews, even though he titled *The Tan Car*, his book of poems, after the poem he wrote at the time of his grandfather's death (Feucht 2003b). "When my grandfather died," Jon says, "I lost someone who was perhaps the most beloved figure in my life, a man who treated me like his grandson, not as his grandson with a disability. To some extent, his death marked the end of my childhood, and I wrote a poem dedicated to him."

If all these deaths, his grandfather's especially, were not enough sadness to endure, Nate, one of Jon's long-time friends but someone he also had not mentioned before, committed suicide the next May. Jon says he was "saddened beyond words by Nate's death." At this point Jon did not see how he could go on with the AVA camp the following summer. Besides, by April he had received only one paid application—he had gotten a lot of inquiries, but only one followed through. Fortunately, by the time the camp rolled around he ended up with 11 paying participants and the camp went on.

Never to rest on his past accomplishments, Jon says that he "wanted this camp to be even better than the first." But with nearly twice as many youths to accommodate, the logistical challenges were more complicated. Jon admits to feeling a lot of pressure and getting a little short with the support staff when things didn't go well, even with something as small as not having the bedding ready in the dorms when the campers arrived on the first day.

> I can be kind of an alpha male, always wanting to dominate and be in control, and I have trouble delegating responsibilities to others, especially if they seem to carry out these responsibilities in a lackadaisical manner. Then there was the mother of one of the campers who complained about everything—from the dorm accommodations to the prohibition against smoking in the buildings. On the second day of camp she came up to me and said they were leaving. I said, "I'm sorry, but we're not club med." I'm sure she left thinking I was a jerk, but everyone was happier when she was gone. On top of this, two of the campers came without attendants, so we had to use our counselors as aides. One of the kids had an attention deficit disorder issue, which was difficult to handle, especially because we weren't prepared to work with that type of person.
>
> On the bright side there was Kim, a woman with cerebral palsy who was an advanced AAC user whom we hired from California to come and teach the kids. We had a romantic attraction to each other, but nothing ever became of it. Another bright spot was Derek. He was exactly the type of person I had in mind as the model student for the camp—very bright and witty. Derek was from Minnesota and a Vikings football fan, while I am a diehard Green Bay Packers fan, and we loved ribbing each other about whose team was better. I truly believe that Derek had the ability to live his life on his own, so I was disappointed when I heard his parents decided to place him in a group home. Even if those of us with significant disabilities need paid caregivers to maintain our independence, I think it's better to live on our own, without the paternalistic security of an institutional living situation. Ideally, that's what I want the campers who pass through AVA to strive for. I realize that everyone can't succeed in an independent living situation, but at least they should give it a good try before they resign themselves to a more dependent existence.

Jon once talked about this issue in a speech he gave upon receiving the Edwin and Esther Prentke AAC Distinguished Lecturer Award in 2003:

Why do we act like our work is done when we get somebody communicating
effectively? Our work is not done at that point; it's just beginning. It's like
finding a penny on the ground and thinking that you are set for life? Do we
celebrate every time able-bodied people talk? Of course not, it's part of everyday life.

I know many parents and educators who are so happy to have their child be
able to just express their needs. I think people who do this are doing a great
disservice to their child, because there is so much more to life and communication than just expressing needs. We need to teach children and adults how to
communicate their feelings and ideas; by doing this, we get to see their personality and start to understand who they are. I believe that besides teaching our
children how to communicate, we need to teach them three fundamental values
of communication. . . . First, they need to know how to use communication to
function in mainstream America. . . . Second, we need to teach them how to
use communication to get ahead in life. . . . Third, we need to teach them how
to use communication to make their mark on the world. (2003a)

The sentiments Jon expressed in this speech are related to one of the disap-
pointments he feels about disability services at UW-Whitewater.

I know some people who have gone through the program who just sit around,
collect their social security disability insurance, and live like hermits, playing
video games and drinking and smoking pot. They don't go out into the world
to make a difference, for themselves or others. I think the downside of services
that are nowadays available for people with disabilities is that it can make
things a little too cushy for some people—they get too used to being taken care
of, of having accommodations made for them, rather than striving for their
shot at the American dream.[1]

The year between the second and third AVA camp, Jon's last year as an
undergraduate, continued to be a tumultuous time for him. A couple of the
staff who had helped him with the first two camps, and whom he liked very
much, left. And then came the news that Dick Lee would be leaving at the
end of the 2002–2003 academic year. Jon started to doubt whether he could
continue the camp without Dick, because of both his personal and financial
support.

Around this time, too, Jon had gotten romantically involved with his good
friend Stasia. Stasia has cerebral palsy, and she and Jon had met when Stasia's mother had asked Jon to assist with her high school Individualized
Education Plan.[2]

We became best friends, and I helped her get into Whitewater. I also became
quite close with her mother. But when Stasia came home with a hickey one
day, her mother got very upset and stopped speaking to me. To make matters
worse, earlier that year I had asked Stasia to prepare a Straight Talk to give at

the 2003 camp. I know how long it can take to prepare a computerized talk, and when she hadn't even started it just a few weeks before the camp, I pulled her off the program. We had a big blowout and that cemented the end to our relationship.

Following this, Jon also had a brief sexual relationship with a neighbor woman he met when he was out for a walk one day. "We got to talking, one thing led to another, and we had sex a couple of times over the course of a weekend. She was bipolar and very unstable, and for some reason—I'm still not sure why—she called the police on me."

In spite of this turmoil, both Dick's departure and the emotionality of the two sexual relationships, Jon managed to graduate in May, a major milestone in his life. It had taken him seven years. "Growing up," Jon says, "few people thought I could do it. But I proved them wrong." Graduation day was a momentous day for both Jon and his family, and he wrote a poem to commemorate the event.

As for AVA, Jon never told anyone he was having doubts about its viability, because he thought they would try to talk him out of quitting. But on the first day of the 2003 camp, Jon found himself laughing with a couple of the campers. "It really felt good," Jon recalls, "because it was the first time in a long time that I had laughed so naturally. I started to realize that AVA, like everything else in life, would have its highs and lows."

One downside of the 2003 camp, however, was a run-in Jon had with Nadia, one of the camp counselors. One of the campers had gotten burned in the shower with hot water because he was left unattended, and she accused Jon of being responsible and not caring about what happened. This was the first Jon had heard of it, but she continued to rail against him as if it was his fault. The argument got so heated that one of the other staff members had to separate them before it turned into fisticuffs.

The upside of the camp, on the other hand, was Sarah Faulkner, a 21-year-old camper with cerebral palsy from Toledo, Ohio. Jon and Sarah were attracted to each other right away, and when she returned home, she instant-messaged him, thanking him for a great week and saying she had hated to leave. Before long they started talking to each other day and night—and falling in love. For the most part they carried on their relationship over Webcams for three years, visiting each other on Thanksgivings and during AVA camps, until they got married in 2006.

The first time Jon met Sarah's family was on the first of these Thanksgiving trips. Jon says that Sarah's father, a husky man at 6 feet 5 inches and 320 pounds, is the most kindhearted person he ever met—"unless you get him mad, and in that respect he is very much like me." He even came to the Milwaukee airport to get Jon and fly him back to Ohio. "I remember trying to keep up with him in the airport as he barreled through the crowd. I almost took out a kid in my power chair. My first thought was, 'Holy cow, what did I get myself into?' But he and I have become like father and son." Sarah's mother, on the other hand, "is more difficult to read. She loves everybody around her but seems to lack empathy for problems they may have. She has studied psychology and knows how to get me to relax. But she also knows how to get under my skin; it's in her nature to want to bug people."

Jon says that people have asked him if Sarah's parents were ever concerned about his ability to take care of and provide for their daughter. But Sarah tells them that her parents taught her to be independent and does not need a man to take care of her. Jon's parents, too, readily accepted Sarah into their family. "The only one who gave me a hard time," Jon says, "was Sarah's younger sister Natalie. We have a love/hate relationship. The first time I talked to her on the computer she told me that she'd kick my ass if I didn't treat Sarah right."

Meeting and falling in love with Sarah was a turning point in Jon's life. "I cannot overstate," Jon says, "how she saved me." But even Sarah couldn't stave off the demons that were haunting him. In retrospect he thinks that his bipolar condition, undiagnosed at the time, had a lot to do with the way he handled conflict. He tended to overreact if he thought somebody was out to get him, which only escalated the conflict. If something was not going right, his mind would start racing out of control and he would panic and work himself into a sweat. "I felt like I was living my life with one foot on the gas pedal and the other foot on the brakes," Jon explains, "and I was drinking quite a lot, even drove my wheelchair home drunk from the bars a couple of times."

Then, in January 2004, Jon got very sick with a severe cold and flu that turned into pneumonia. He stopped eating and had to be hospitalized. He was given heavy doses of medication and was in a daze. When he finally recovered from the pneumonia, the doctors said he also should be treated for depression, and they prescribed medication for that. In retrospect it was the wrong diagnosis, and the side effects of the medication only made Jon worse. When he started feeling suicidal, Jon was rational enough to know to ask for help. He called the police and admitted himself into a hospital psych ward. Over the next few years he was hospitalized a total of seven times, the first two times for a week, but the other times for just 24 hours. During those periods of hospitalization, he participated in individual and group therapy, and they adjusted his medications to try to get him back on the right track.

Of this time in his life, Jon says that the stigma about possibly having a "mental illness" was hard to take.

> It's difficult enough having a physical disability like mine, but there's nothing that scares other people more than learning you were in a "nut house." And people have no idea what goes on in these places, assuming that everyone's in

a straightjacket or that we're all mass murderers. For years I hid the pain and shame, and I was riddled with self-doubt, feeling like the amazing Jon Feucht was a fraud. And I was paranoid that I'd be placed in a residential facility or group home because of my out-of-control temper.

It was not until 2011 that I was actually diagnosed with bipolar disorder. At the time I was feeling desperate for an answer to my emotional state. Then, when I saw a television show about a prison inmate who was given a medication to control his temper, I asked my doctor about it. He put me on a low dose of Depakote, which is used for migraines, epilepsy, and bipolar disorder. When I was still losing my temper after that, I went back to see him. At this point he thought about increasing the dose but said it would be better if I saw a psychiatrist.

I made an appointment with a psychiatrist for a month later and started reading up on bipolar disorder. On the day of the appointment I was nervous. Actually, I was scared to death. I told the doctor all about my emotional history going back to high school. Then he asked me to come back with Sarah, because he wanted to ask her a few questions. Two weeks later we all met, and at the end of the hour he said, "Yes, I think you are bipolar." He said he didn't know exactly what type, and that we'd need to experiment a little in order to find the right medication and proper dose that would work best. [3]

When I got home that night I called my parents to tell them the news. I was surprised that my mom wasn't surprised. She had figured this out some time ago. She and I had had epic arguments, but she always knew I couldn't help myself. Hearing her say that was like being released from a prison sentence that had held me locked up for years.

In spite of everything Jon had been going through in the first half of 2004, he pulled himself together enough to pull off the camp, his first one since Dick Lee had left. It was also the first time he had worked with a different speech pathologist, a person he came to detest.

Never in my life had I worked with such an unprofessional pathologist. When we had a fundraiser to raise money for kids to come to the camp, he decided to show a graphic documentary about a woman with cerebral palsy giving birth. Really?!! He had no idea how inappropriate this was. Then he would call my camp staff names, turning to me to say that somebody was a "bitch." I wanted to take him by the shirt, shake him, and tell him "You are the biggest prick I know."

It was during the 2004 camp that Jon's exuberance for AVA began shifting from being *fun* to being *work*. And this feeling carried through to the 2005 camp, when his "dream camper," the type of person he had envisioned for AVA, arrived.

Hannah had everything going for her. She was smart, as driven as I was, and I was licking my chops to have a chance to work with her. But on the morning of the third day of the camp, the camp speech pathologist told me that Hannah wanted to talk. When I went over to her, I was stunned when she told me she was leaving. She told me I had "sold out" by allowing people with cognitive disabilities to come to the camp. She accused me of "false advertising" the camp as a place where people with communicative disabilities could come to develop their skills to pursue a college education. AVA, she said, was not a place for her.

I was devastated, truly hurt by Hannah's departure. Truth be told, I would have preferred to send everyone else home just to be a mentor to her. Everyone else tried to cheer me up, but I felt like my initial dream for the camp was slipping through my fingers and there was nothing I could do about it.

Ironically, Hannah and Jon stayed in touch and he used her as a case study for his master's thesis (Feucht 2006). Like Jon, Hannah has a sense of humor that disarms people's prejudices. She is motivationally driven, thinking she needs to push herself because other people have such low expectations for her. Insofar as she does have minimal ability to use verbal speech, she tends to avoid using assistive technology while at school to speed up her process of communication, and because she thinks the stored messages that can be programmed on speech-generating devices for routine situations do too much of the thinking *for* her rather than let her do the thinking for herself. Stored messages allow users to activate full sentences or even paragraphs categorized by particular topics. Jon, too, has reservations about these types of systems. They are faster to use, but they take away the speaker's individualized voice (Hoag et al. 2004).

At the time Jon was interviewing Hannah for his thesis, she was 15 years old. She told Jon that her self-confidence can fluctuate on a day-to-day basis. On bad days she thinks of herself as disabled. On good days she thinks that to do so is "ignorant because I have so many abilities that others do not and an amazing family and life, and a wonderful future, which I cannot wait to explore. Most days, I see myself as a unique young woman who can defeat any obstacle that life gives me" (Feucht 2006:21).

Jon says that one of the more influential books he read while working on his master's degree in special education was Michael Wehmeyer and Sharon Field's *Self-Determination: Instructional and Assessment Strategies* (2007). Wehmeyer and Field define self-determined behavior as "the attitudes and abilities required to act as the primary causal agent in one's life and to make choices regarding one's actions free from external influence or interference" (p. 2). Hannah is this type of person, as is Jon. "I can't explain why we are the way we are," Jon says, "other than to credit our families. I know I get a lot of my drive from my parents, and this appears to be the case for Hannah, too. I interviewed her mother for my thesis, who told me this about her daughter."

My dreams for Hannah are of course to be happy. From my vantage point now, her being a sophomore, I hope she can go to college independent of her dad and me. Maybe that includes living alone or with roommates. I want her to be productive, working on something she cares about and to enjoy her job every day. As far as her social life, I wish for her to have good friends, date and eventually marry. But not too quickly, I can't imagine a day without Hannah in my house. (Feucht 2006:22)

Not all disabled people, Jon has come to accept, will be capable of this. And this is when he realized that his dream for AVA had to change. Indeed, one of the things that sticks out in his mind about the 2005 camp was a heart-to-heart conversation he had with one of the camper's mother, who told Jon that she kept asking herself "why" her daughter was not as high functioning as he was.

All I could think of telling her was that questions that start with "why" never get answers. Up to that time, I had often tried to figure out the whys of my life—why had I taken to my communication device when most people did not, why I was able to go to college and live on my own. I realize that in comparison to others who have my degree of physical disability, I had lived a rather extraordinary life, with so much more to accomplish, far beyond what most others would have expected of a man with my challenges.

On the last night of the camp, everybody threw Jon and Sarah a "mock wedding," because the campers were not going to be able to attend the real wedding they would be having the following year. Everything was in lime green, Sarah's favorite color, including her wedding dress. "The joke back then," Jon recalls, "was how I hated lime green. So everyone had a good laugh about that. It was a great evening, one of the best of my life!"

The following year, Jon and Sarah got married a month before the 2006 camp. It was a joyous occasion that made him feel whole. Most of the significantly disabled people Jon knows are not married, so for him it was a sign of success. "To be honest," Jon admits, "I don't like that I've thought about it this way, because I am very much in love with Sarah. She completes me; she's the ying to my yang. Everyone thinks we're the perfect couple. Marriage is about somebody accepting everything about you, the good and the bad. Sarah has stuck by me through everything I've gone through, including my issues with bipolar disorder. As I said, she saved my life."

The wedding was held in Toledo on a hot summer day in June, the day of Jon's 29th birthday. It was 99 degrees and he was sweltering in his tuxedo. "I would not say I was nervous," he recalls. "I had tears in my eyes because I was so happy. For the most part I was in a daze and don't remember much about it. I'm glad we have photos to bring back the memories."

The wedding was followed by the camp, and Jon gave a Straight Talk about how he had found the love of his life, which the campers thoroughly enjoyed. It was also the first year they held a dance at the end of the camp, which the campers just loved, too. Like the previous camps, this one had its highs and lows.

> One of the bright sides of that camp was Kadee, who was 11 years old at the time. Sarah noticed that while Kadee and her mother were playing a board game of Guess Who?, Kadee wasn't using her communication device. When Sarah inquired about this, Kadee looked at her mom to explain. Kadee's mom said that Kadee had problems with her shoulders slipping out of the socket and was unable to hold the device with her arms. I was listening in on the conversation, as was one of the camp counselors, and we came up with the idea of duct-taping Kadee's device to her knees, so she could input her commands with it stabilized in that way. It worked! Kadee was able to communicate with her device to her mom for the first time! We cried because we were so happy.
>
> One camper named Keegan really touched my heart, too. He told me he was amazed at how much I had accomplished, comparing me to John Lennon as far as being a visionary. When people say things like that, I am truly appreciative but also uncomfortable. Inside at that time I was a wreck, and I couldn't understand why people loved me.
>
> The downside of that camp was a new kid who got so homesick that he tried to fake a heart attack to get us to send him home. We didn't want to give in to him and become enablers for him learning he could always get his way. And another of our "veteran" campers, who had been a great kid the years before, started acting out of control and suicidal. When I told him we were going to have to call his parents to take him home, he threw his cell phone at me. I guess he didn't think I was so amazing.

Jon received his master's degree in 2008, but in spite of this accomplishment, he felt a letdown. "I think I feel empty," Jon explains, "when I'm not striving for a goal, and I used school and AVA to escape from my feelings of self-doubt, channeling my anxieties into something positive." Still, Jon thinks he wrote some of his best speeches during the early years of the camp when he was going to school (Feucht 2004). In one, he told the campers that they should not settle for simply making short statements when using their speaking devices. "People won't be able to know how intelligent you are if all you say is 'yes' and 'no,'" he tells them. So one of his "goals for the camp is to get the kids to engage in conversations, to get practice with the nuances of give-and-take exchanges. Even though they'll find people who lack the patience to talk to them, they should not give up. They should try to make others realize what they're missing, that they are not invisible, that they can't be dismissed as irrelevant." Jon also assures the campers that they will, in fact, find people who will be patient enough to sit and talk with them for hours.

Seize the opportunities. Learn from the people who will talk to you and teach them, too. There are so many people, disabled and nondisabled alike, who never express themselves, never share their ideas with others because they're afraid of a negative reaction, afraid that others will think they're dumb. Take a chance. That's the only way to make your way in the world. This includes talking to strangers. To be sure, you will run into people who are afraid of you, who will ignore you or walk away from you, who think you are inferior and who talk down to you and treat you like a child, if they acknowledge your existence at all. But I love watching them open up when they realize that I'm a person just like them, as smart *as* them, or frankly in some cases, smarter *than* them.

Jon also tries teaching the campers to be self-advocates, to learn how to go about getting what they need, to know their legal rights, and to learn how to access the people and resources that can help them. "I don't want them to think that needing to rely on others diminishes their self-worth," Jon says. "Everyone relies on other people for help, whether its family and friends; teachers, coaches and ministers; healthcare and other professionals; or the kindness of strangers." Jon offers the same advice about homecare workers.[4]

These people are essential for our independence, and often we have a love/hate relationship with them. You have to communicate your needs. If they do something you don't like, or aren't doing something they should be doing, don't let things slide. Your resentment will only fester. Tell them politely and matter-of-factly that you didn't really care for what they did or didn't do, and ask if you can discuss how to do things differently.

Additionally, Jon raises the question of whether or not it is a good idea to become friends with your homecare workers, or if it is better to keep the relationship purely on a professional footing.

I've been on both sides of this issue, and there is no right or wrong approach. The main thing to keep in mind is that the homecare industry is funded by the government and that being a homecare worker is one of the lowest paid occupations in society; and we should not take for granted that this industry can remain financially viable when legislators are cutting budgets for disability services.

Perhaps the most important lesson Jon tries to impart to young people is encapsulated in what he calls the "four D's"—drive, desire, determination, and demand.

Drive entails the question of ambition, the motivation to do something. It's what gets you out of bed in the morning to carry on with life. *Desire* is similar but entails the fire in the belly that you get when you really want to do something. *Determination* is the ability to push on and on until you accomplish your goal. For disabled people it requires a strong work ethic and degree of persistence beyond what is required of nondisabled people. *Demand* refers to asking the very best of yourself, to not settling for less because you have a disability. Do not be deterred by other people's low expectations, and don't internalize these expectations. Find the people who believe in you and get the support you need. Seek out people with disabilities who can help show you by example how to accomplish the things that you think are impossible. Expect to encounter obstacles along the way, but think of these as challenges that can be solved rather than as insurmountable barriers.

Lastly, Jon tries to teach the campers the importance of authenticity: "Say what you mean and mean what you say, and expect others to do the same." At the same time, Jon advises them to be open to personal growth and change. "Take each day as an opportunity to learn something new, to assimilate new information and ways of seeing the world and yourself." And this goes for the use of assistive technology.

Be open to updating your assistive technology. Personally I used to be very bullheaded about the assistive technology that I used. I'd try something once and if it didn't work perfectly I'd stop using it. But I learned to not be afraid of trying something new, and to try it over and over again. But don't do this if it's just to acquire the latest gadget or to look cool. The innovation we seek is not cosmetic; it is functionality not appearances that we're after. I myself am addicted to the idea of making progress, of not getting too comfortable with where I'm at. But that's not for everybody. If you're happy with the niche you've found in life, I'm fine with that. But if you want something more, don't hesitate to go for it!

NOTES

1. See Berger (2009).
2. An IEP includes a description of a child's current levels of performance, "annual goals and short-term objectives . . . to target during the coming year, . . . the services and specialized instruction to be provided . . . and how they will be provided," the amount of time the child will spend in a regular classroom setting, and the criteria and methods that will be used to evaluate progress (Marshak, Seligman, and Prezant 1999:119).
3. See Chapter 2, note 4.
4. See Meyer, Donelly, and Weerakoon (2007); Wedgwood (2011).

Jon and Sarah's wedding (2006). Permission by Jon and Sarah Feucht.

Jon and Sarah (2006). Permission by Jon and Sarah Feucht.

Jon with parents, Janet and Al (2006). Permission by Jon Feucht.

Jon with sister Janeen and brother Jeff (2006). Permission by Jon Feucht.

Jon and Sarah on vacation in San Francisco (2011). Permission by Jon and Sarah Feucht.

Part 2

Participant Observation

Chapter Five

Authentic Voices of America: A Relational Ethnography

Earlier we noted that Jon's story should not be viewed as some invariant "truth," but rather as an expression of his self-understanding, of how he sees himself and wants others to see him. As such, his life history gives us one point of entry into the lived experience of a person with a significant disability. We noted, too, our intention to use participant observation as part of a mixed methods approach aimed at broadening understanding of our subject matter.

In this and the following chapter we offer ethnographic accounts of Ron's involvement with Jon in social milieus that provide additional windows into the world of disability and augmentative-alternative communication. Our approach is indicative of what D. Jean Clandinin refers to as "relational ethnography," as Ron became part of Jon's world and Jon a part of Ron's, and where the aim of the inquiry was not to generate a "representation of a reality independent of the knower," but rather to offer a narrative account that gives the reader a sense of the lived experience of what the observer is observing (2013:14). In doing so, Ron also adopted what Christina Papadimitriou describes as the two-prong approach characteristic of "phenomenological seeing": a reflexive movement of looking inward to clear himself of ableist biases, and an empathic movement of looking outward to the world of disability in order to listen and faithfully record what he sees as transpiring (2001:216, 2008b).[1]

The occasion for the observations narrated in this chapter was the five-day Authentic Voices of America camp held at the University of Wisconsin-Whitewater in the summer of 2011. Although this was the eleventh camp in the history of AVA, it was Ron's first camp and also his first opportunity to see and interact with Jon outside of an "interview" situation. Before the start of the camp, Jon told Ron that in addition to simply observing the camp, he should try to engage the campers in conversation to give them additional opportunities to speak with their computerized devices. To more faithfully represent the phenomenology of what Ron observed, this account is narrated in Ron's first-person voice as a *temporally unfolding experience.* This mode of representation will enable readers to follow Ron's perceptual evolution from an attitude of unfamiliarity to an attitude of nonchalance, whereby disability differences that were at one time new to him became commonplace (see Miller and Sammons 1999). [2]

DAY ONE

It was a hot summer day, and the registration table for the camp was set up outdoors because the Knilans Hall dormitory where the campers would be staying was not air-conditioned and was hot and stuffy. Most of the campers and their families rolled up in vans. A few got out of their vehicles and walked on their own accord, but most rolled out of the back of the vans in power wheelchairs, exiting the vehicles on ramps. Some of the campers, who range from 13 to 23 years of age, came with two parents, some with one parent, some with one parent and an attendant, and some with an attendant only. In one case two parents dropped off their child with an attendant and then left for the week. The youths, 18 in all, have traveled from more than a dozen states, from as far as Colorado, Arkansas, New York, and Connecticut. Most if not all of them have cerebral palsy, but one of the campers also has autism and another has a brain injury, in addition to CP. Some of the campers are "veterans," as the camp counselors call them, having attended the camp in previous years. Others are "rookies."

Registration was completed at 4:30 p.m., upon which the campers met in the basement of Knilans Hall for an orientation led by the camp coordinator Dan Price. [3] Dan, who uses a manual wheelchair for mobility, is a former wheelchair basketball player and current coach in the UWW wheelchair basketball program. Dan and his able-bodied assistants, Jake and Janice, easily established rapport with the youths. Dan and Jake, in comradely masculine style, did this with friendly bantering. Many high fives and fist bumps were exchanged. "How's my main man?" "You're the man." A lot of friendly ribbing made the campers feel comfortable and evoked laughter. "Are you going to give me a hard time this week?" Dan ribbed Michelle. Teasing about rival sports teams was a common rapport-building strategy. Gene is from Ohio, and his favorite football team is the Cincinnati Bengals. "The Bengals suck," Jake teased. "Go Packers!"

I tried to start up a conversation with Trent, who was accompanied by his father and Trent's service dog Shine, a regal golden retriever. Trent, who is in his early twenties, lives with his parents and is not particularly adept at using his AAC device. He is able to communicate to his family through gestures and utterances, the words of which are intelligible to those familiar with his speech patterns. This is the reason, his father said, Trent is not very motivated to learn how to use his device, because in the company of his family he can get by without it.

Trent's father prompted Trent to respond to me with his device. I said something about Shine being an awesome dog, that I once had a golden retriever, too. Trent tried to type something on his AAC device, but he had trouble doing so. His father said that Trent thinks that Shine is a "chick magnet." We all laughed. I looked forward to Day Two, the first full day of camp.

DAY TWO

Breakfast with the campers was too early for me, so I joined them at 9:00 a.m. in the air-conditioned building across the street from Knilans Hall. The morning will be divided between Jon's "Straight Talk" session and a "Language Time" session led by speech pathologist Lauren Zubow. The campers will be separated into two groups, with one group going to Jon's Straight Talk and the other to Lauren's Language Time. Then, after about an hour or so, the campers will take a break and switch groups. Today I decided to skip Language Time and listen to both Straight Talks.

Jon positioned himself in the front of the room, and speaking through his AAC device said that he was resurrecting a speech he had given at his first AVA camp in 2001. The speech was prerecorded, but Jon stopped periodically to engage the youths in discussion. "We are going to discuss what it really means to be disabled," he said. After a few more sentences, he asked the audience what they thought it meant to be disabled. The responses were slow in coming. It takes a long time for inexperienced AAC users to type their messages. For campers who are severely quadriplegic, I was amazed to learn that some of them use a device that is activated by scanning the computer screen that is attached to their wheelchairs with the retina of their eyes. This takes a lot of practice, and time, to operate.

Up to this point I did not yet know all the campers by name, and even after I learned them it was a little difficult to tell who was speaking in these group sessions. But the first camper I heard who completed his response to the question about what it means to be disabled said, "Using a wheelchair." Another said, "Using my Tobii," referring to the brand name of the device she uses. This was not a very talkative group of youths, and there were no more responses. Later I learned that this was a less advanced group than the other one that attended Jon's second Straight Talk session.

After a pause, Jon continued with his speech. He wanted the campers to know that they can have "any job in the world." They can "become doctors, lawyers, and the President of the United States." I thought to myself that President of the United States is a stretch, but it was followed by a more important message: "When somebody tells you that you can't do something because you are disabled, don't listen. . . . I don't want you to say down the road, 'Why did I listen to this person?' And that goes for listening to parents too. You very well may be the only disabled person they know. Like you, they don't know what's out there for people like us."[4]

With that, Jon asked if there were any questions. One of the campers said, "No." After a pause, a parent asked, "Were you always motivated to communicate with people?" Jon said "yes." I surmised that the sentiment behind the question must be that some youths are not so motivated. Later I asked Jon about this, and he said he knows this is the case, but he is not sure why. Perhaps Trent's father had a partial answer. But it could also be the inherent difficulty in learning how to use the device, especially when there is little institutional support for the technical assistance that is needed to set up and maintain the equipment. Thus research finds that it is common for users to stop using their device because it fails to deliver the desired results.[5]

Another parent asked Jon about the type of device he uses, and a discussion ensued among the parents about the types of devices their children use. Then we took a break, and resumed shortly thereafter with the second group. This time the audience was positioned in a circle, with Jon in the middle. Jon wanted to begin, but Allison, who I later learned has both CP and autism, was spinning her power wheelchair in circles adjacent to Jon, and he asked her to stop. Allison's mother for some reason was not with us at the moment, so another "veteran" parent who seemed to know Allison pushed her chair to the edge of the circle and asked her to settle down.

Jon changed the script from the first session and said he wanted to talk about what it means to live independently. Perhaps he was anticipating that the youths in this group will be more talkative, which they were. He asked the campers, "What are a couple of things you want to do in your life?" Allison responded, "Pop Warner football," referring to the disabled recreational activity she is involved in. Jon replied, "Football is a challenge." Other campers said "power soccer," "swimming," and "bowling." Another said, "I like baseball." Diane said, "Weaving. I make tapestry. Scarves." Still others said: "Get a job." "I want to work for ESPN." "I want to go to college." "I want to make people with CP walk." Dahlia's simple and direct response hit home with me: "I want to talk to you." This, it seemed to me, best answers the earlier question about people's motivation to use the device. It expresses the most basic human need to make a connection with another person. Then Jon returned to the theme of what it means to be disabled. "What do you think?" he asked the youths. Someone said, "I feel embarrassed." Neil said,

"People are so dumb?," referring to the way in which nondisabled people respond to him. Regarding his AAC device, Neil added, "It is hard to have a disability because people don't understand how to treat it."

Soon thereafter we took a break for lunch and moved to the dining hall downstairs. The cafeteria was filled with youths who were on campus for other specialty camps involving sports and music. Lacrosse, tennis, and percussion were the ones that came to my attention. And then there were the cheerleaders. For the most part, during mealtimes, the nondisabled students seemed to ignore the disabled campers. But the parents and I noticed the rudeness of the cheerleaders, who exuded annoyance that disabled people in power wheelchairs were taking up their privileged space, forcing them to step aside to make room for the chairs and slowing up the cafeteria line. We thought of them as mean girls *par excellence*. But they did not need to fear for long, as we ate in a separate dining room adjacent to the main cafeteria.

Most of the campers, Jon included, cannot feed themselves. I watched, for the first time in my life, as parents and their aides fed them. Some have difficulty swallowing, so they can only eat soft foods. Jon even brought along an Osterizer, which his paid aide used to blend some of his food. Some campers were fed a liquid diet through a feeding tube in their stomachs.

I struck up conversations with the campers and parents. I found myself feeling impressed with the parents' devotion to their children, but also how, as Katie's mother told me, that "being disabled is a full-time job," adding that when she first learned that her daughter had CP it was like "getting punched in the stomach." Peter's mother said that having a child with a disability "changes your life." She seemed tired, even a little depressed. At a meal later in the week Doreen's mother said her doctor once suggested that she should just let her daughter die; other medical professionals thought she should have Doreen institutionalized.

All this made me wonder about the elements of the disability rights movement that aim to counter social oppression by "celebrating" disability as an affirmative identity and valued form of social diversity (Baker 2011; Barnes and Mercer 2001; Gilson and DePoy 2000). This orientation is based on a minority group model of disability pride that positions disability alongside other oppositional movements based on race/ethnicity, gender, and sexual orientation. This model is no doubt apt because, as Neil's comments suggested, the challenges faced by people with disabilities are most assuredly exacerbated by interpersonal prejudice and institutional discrimination. At the same time, it seems facile to deny that the impairments are real and constitute an element of the disability experience that cannot be reduced to social context, however crucial and in some cases determinative this context may be (Bury 2000; Hughes and Paterson 1997; Shakespeare 2010; Thomas 2004).

After lunch and another break the campers swam at the campus pool, and in the evening they bowled at the campus bowling alley. I was unable to attend these activities, but would return the next day.

DAY THREE

On day three I decided to start my morning with the Language Time session led by speech pathologist Lauren Zubow. Lauren is among a minority in her profession who knows how to use an AAC device, and I soon learned she is a very skilled teacher as well.

Lauren stood in the front of the room by a map of the United States and began by asking each camper to verbalize the name of the state they were from. She then asked them to come up and locate their state on the map. A second exercise involved a computerized "Mad Lib" activity where the campers were asked to fill in a requested particle of speech. The youths completed three Mad Libs—a Letter from Camp, a Love Letter, and a Sick Note—after which Lauren played the response on her computer. This evoked much joyous laughter that was wonderful to see.

After the break, I accompanied these campers to Jon's Straight Talk session. Jon opened with a line from a Jimmy Buffet song: "Come Monday it will be all right." He recalled that when he first heard this song he thought it said "Come what may it will be all right." Then Jon told the campers that they "need to work hard to make everything all right." Jon said that he never gave up, even if it took him years to work out his problems. Later Jon would admit to me that he still hadn't worked out all of his problems. "Always have hope," Jon advised the youths. Then he asked, "Have any of you ever given up hope?" When there were no responses, Jon said, "Campers, you need to communicate more."

Suddenly a mother raised her hand and asked Jon to slow down. "Cody had started to write his response," she said, "but he didn't have enough time to finish." Jon shook his head acknowledging his error. I found this exchange particularly interesting, because timing in conversational exchanges is an issue that AAC users often face with nondisabled listeners who don't have the patience to wait for them to complete their thoughts; the listener tends to fill in the gaps and complete their sentences before they have a chance to finish (Hodge 2007). One has to learn to appreciate these delays, and being a person who relishes the calm moments of time, I had already become acclimated to the pace, which can be a relaxing form of exchange. I have found that some nondisabled people sometimes speak before they think, that is, they start talking as a way to figure out what they really want to say. AAC users have to give more prior thought to what they say and make every word count.

The inexperienced AAC user, however, may make input errors that confuse the communication. In response to Jon's question about hope, it took time for Allison to input her intended response. She said something about the time her power chair was broken and it took a long time to fix. At the same time, she knew it would get fixed. But the actual words that came out of Allison's device did not communicate this information clearly, and her mother had to translate Allison's thoughts in a way that was intelligible to the rest of us.

Then we heard from Neil: "I never give up." And Cody: "I want to keep trying." Jon asked if anyone ever gave up something they later regretted. The campers' responses indicated they had not. Instead they offered examples of not giving up. Darlene: "Walking in my walker." Cody: "Working on a second chance for college." Jon reiterated that "no life is without problems" and offered the adage: "When one door closes, another one opens." Dahlia added, "People with a disability can do whatever they want, but they have to work harder." At the end of the session Cody told Jon, "Thank you for your words."

At the lunch break I decided to eat with Cody and his mother Stella. Stella mentioned the time at a previous camp that Jon had told Cody that he had the ability to go to college. It was an epiphany for Cody. "One sentence," she said, "changed his life." Stella explained that Cody had been enrolled in a community college in Illinois but had dropped out. Now he wanted to attend UWW. Cody told me that the "people [at the college] were mean." Thinking he was referring to the students, I said that the students at UWW are more sensitive to disability issues and that I didn't think he would have those problems here. Cody clarified that he wasn't referring to the students but to the staff, including someone who told him: "We're working so hard for you. I don't want you to end up alone in a room." I winced. I found myself liking Cody a lot, drawn to him more than any other camper. He is a smart young man who wants to make a difference. I wanted to get to know him better.

After lunch the campers were scheduled for arts and crafts. Jon said he wanted to talk about some things that were troubling him about the camp, and we found a quiet place in the UWW student center. He told me about a mother of one of the campers who had told him that he was an "inspiration" to her daughter. This was not the first time someone has said something like this to Jon. But Jon said he was feeling that he doesn't deserve this accolade, that people were expecting him to be a type of person he is not. This was the first time Jon had opened up to me about his psychological troubles, including his suffering from a generalized anxiety disorder and depression (only later learning that his primary symptoms were due to a bipolar condition). He has had issues with anger management and periodically gets into a "dark place," even has had suicidal thoughts. He has been hospitalized in a "psych ward" a few times. "I want to tell you this," Jon said, "because it shows the true Jon Feucht lives hard." Later he told me that he did not get to where he is today by simply working hard, but by "being an egotist," having to be so focused on becoming successful that he sometimes isolated himself from his family, the ones he loves. Jon said that since earning his master's degree in 2008, he has felt as if he has reached a plateau in his life that sometimes makes him feel empty. The more formal education and degrees he has achieved, the more striking is the gap between his accomplishments and strangers' stereotypes of a man in a wheelchair who can't speak without a machine. They think he's "cognitively disabled," and he wonders whether this is what the AVA campers have to look forward to as well, even under the best of circumstances. He has even contemplated leaving AVA.

I told Jon that this reality of his life makes him a more realistic role model for disabled youths, that I did not think his flaws and self-doubts undermine the positive influence he has had (and will continue to have) on others. If some people put him on a pedestal, it makes him an unattainable role model they can't emulate. If he is a real person with real problems, others might more easily relate to him as a person like themselves. I said these things to Jon, but I wasn't sure if he was consoled.

DAY FOUR

The fourth day of camp revolved around an afternoon field trip to the Milwaukee Brewers baseball game. There was no Straight Talk today, but before we departed Lauren held a Language Time with all of the campers together. She put a series of pictures on the board, one by one, asking the youths to describe what they saw. The pictures moved from a small part of a larger whole to progressively broader vantage points until the entire picture was in view. The campers offered anywhere from one word to two sentence answers. Following this exercise, Lauren divided the campers into several small groups and asked them to tell each other two things that were true about themselves, and one thing that was a lie; the other campers were supposed to guess which was the lie.

At 11:00 a.m. we boarded three large school buses with wheelchair lifts. I got on the third bus with five campers and their parents. For some reason Jon did not join us. His wife Sarah, whom I had not met before this camp, also uses an AAC device and a power wheelchair, said, "He has stuff to do." On our way to the ballpark I talked to Craig's father, Jerry. Jerry lives in Indiana and he told me that Craig would like to attend college at UWW. But finances are an obstacle, not only the out-of-state tuition but also the cost of attendant care. And even if the money issues can be resolved, Jerry wondered if it would be financially worthwhile given the challenges Craig will inevitably face obtaining employment following graduation. Jerry brought up Indiana

Governor Mitch Daniels, austerity budget involving tax cuts for the wealthy funded in part by cuts in social services for people like Craig. I commiserated that we were experiencing the same thing with Governor Scott Walker in Wisconsin.[6]

Later I would ask Jon what he thought about this. While he was reluctant to criticize austerity-oriented politicians, who he thinks are looking out for small business people like his parents, he was aware of his own (somewhat ambiguous) class status. For his daily expenses and healthcare he relies on public assistance: Social Security Disability Insurance, Medicare, and Medicaid, supplemented by a county medical insurance program. But his parents have been able to pay for his college education without having to go into debt, and they have purchased a nice wheelchair accessible home in Whitewater for Sarah and him to live in. In this respect Jon enjoys a relatively privileged life in comparison to so many other people with disabilities, and he describes himself as "richly poor," the title of a poem he wrote a few years ago before he married Sarah (Feucht 2003b). At the same time, he regrets that his dependency on government assistance limits his ability to become more financially independent. To maintain his services, particularly his attendant care and healthcare benefits, he is only allowed to earn a limited amount of money. If he earns more, he loses his benefits, making it financially infeasible for him to seek more financially remunerative employment. This, too, fuels Jon's doubts about deceiving the campers about what the future holds for them. As he lamented, "I say push yourself, make success work, go to college. But for what? The government doesn't want people with disabilities actually working . . . [at least] not at a middle-class level."

After we arrived at the ballpark, the campers boarded one of two elevators that took us to our seats. I was pleasantly surprised at how smoothly this went. Dan Price had reserved a last row in the leftfield bleachers, which is accessible to wheelchairs and has a few folding chairs for the rest of us to sit in. We arrived as the Brewers came to the plate in the bottom of the first inning. The leadoff batter Cory Hart hit a homerun that landed about a dozen rows below us. The campers were excited as the crowd cheered loudly. Later a few would say that the field trip was the highlight of the entire week.

DAY FIVE

On the last day of camp I arrived at 9:00 a.m. for Jon's Straight Talk session. Apparently there would be no Language Time today, as Jon wanted to address everyone together as one group. On the board in front of the room was a list of four items that anticipated what Jon would be speaking about: (1) hero worship, (2) reverse side of success, (3) family, and (4) putting priorities first. Maybe this is what Jon was working on yesterday while we were all at the game.

I noticed that Sarah was crying and I expected an emotional talk, hoping that Jon had not decided to leave AVA. Jon began by saying that this talk will be "like nothing I've done before." Then he asked, "How many of you think I'm a hero or role model?" There was not much of a response. Then Jon motioned to Eric's father Mark, who has agreed to play some music that Jon has requested. Mark turned on his player and we listened to "Superman," a song about how it's not easy to be the man people think you are. When the song was over, I wasn't sure if the campers had understood the song's meaning. But then Jon said something reminiscent of our conversation the other day:

> I do appreciate you looking up to me. But it's important to not make me into something I'm not. Nobody wins when I'm looked upon as a hero. It doesn't work. Yes it might seem like I make everything look easy. But nothing is easy. I think about the years I had written so many speeches and I will always do that. But today I need to give everybody a reality check. Life is not easy and the more success you go after the more problems you make yourself vulnerable to.

Next Jon asked, "How many campers and their parents would like themselves to have my life or parts of my life?" A few slowly raised their hands. Jon motioned to Mark to play another song, "Be Like That," which is about thinking that your life would be better if you could live in another's shoes. Again, I wasn't sure if the song had the effect on the group that Jon hoped for. But he then moved on to the second part of his talk: "Now the reverse side of success. Does anybody know what I mean?" Someone, I could not tell whom, said "more responsibilities." Gene, who I have learned is one of the brightest youths in the camp, said, "failure." Jon added, "Every day Sarah and I leave the house to do our business and most days people talk down to us and that deflates me personally." With this remark Jon turned the conversation to the question of "adversity." Gene said, "The road to success is paved with adversity."

By now the Straight Talk session has gone on for well over an hour. From the back of the room, Dan rolled forward in his wheelchair and said it was time to take a break. As the group temporarily disbanded, Dan and Lauren talked to Jon about what to do with the remainder of the morning. Dan thought that 90 percent of what Jon was saying was going over the heads of the campers, and he reminded him that the main point of the camp was to get the youths to talk, not to impart a philosophy of life, however important that may be. Jon realized Dan was right. He was disappointed, even angry, at the response (or, rather, the lack of response) to his talk. He felt he had taken a risk in saying what he said, but he agreed that it was best if Lauren took over with a Language Time session.

Jon's use of song had given Lauren an idea, and she proceeded to ask the campers to tell the group about their favorite songs. This led to a fascinating exchange. Gene mentioned "I've Got a Feeling," and Andrew said "Elvis." Doreen's favorite song was "Somewhere Over the Rainbow." Her device is capable of playing music, and her attendant played us the rendition by Israel Kamakawiwo 'Ole, one of my favorites too. Michelle and Katie mentioned religious songs, "Casting Crowns" and "Amazing Grace," respectively. Diane said "Circle Game," and her father played the Joni Mitchell tune for us.

Eric, who fashions himself as a budding comedian, mentioned "What Is This Feeling?" from the *Wicked* musical.[7] Eric is an able-bodied walker and one of the fastest AAC users in the camp. Later Jon would say that after having lunch with Eric he "went home tired" because he "couldn't keep up with his speed." With a big grin on his face, Eric played us his favorite song about "loathing." With this, everyone laughed. Lauren asked Eric why he liked the song. Because it "makes Dad crazy," he said. Craig followed with Jimmy Buffet's "Fruitcakes." When Lauren asked him how the song made him feel, Craig said, "happy go lucky." For a change of pace, Cody said he liked "jazz," for "working and writing"—another reason I became fond of this young man.

Then Darlene raised some eyebrows when she mentioned Eminem's "Not Afraid," a song about letting people know that you're not alone and not allowing others stop you from "causing mayhem." Not to be outdone, Allison said she liked "Lady Gaga." Megan, an able-bodied walker who appeared rather adept with her AAC device and smart phone, wanted to play us Jay Sean's "All or Nothing," a song about summer love. With great joy she moved rhythmically to the lively beat as the other campers (and parents) followed suit. Perhaps this, I thought, is what it means to celebrate disability as a valued form of diversity. But Peter stole the show when he selected a song called "Speak to the Angels."[8] Peter is arguably the most cognitively disabled youth in the camp, but he is also among the most engaging, wanting to make a friendly connection with the people around him. I had tears in my eyes as Peter looked lovingly at his mother and sister as the lyrics played: "When you talk to me, you speak the language of the angels."

Lauren changed gears and asked the youths about the strategies they use to make themselves feel better, asking "What lifts your spirits?" Gary answered, "put on some music," and Darlene said she likes her music "loud." Doreen mentioned "red up," which her mother explained was their term for cleaning house. Doreen also said "talk with mom." Trent likes to talk to his sister, and Neil likes to eat. Diane said "macaroni," and Gene "pizza." Dahlia likes to dance, and Cody works on his writing. Jon likes to "go fishing," and Neil wondered how he does it.

Next Lauren asked another question: "What's a good *new* way to make yourself feel better after camp is over?" When no one answered, she asked, "What do you have in *this* room that can help?" When Diane said "friend," Lauren added, "reach out to a new friend." She then asked, "What are some things that you love about camp?" Neil, Gene, and Allison liked the ball-game. Andrew said he "learned to appreciate air-conditioning." Darlene said she "learned about all different communication devices," and Dahlia said she learned how to use her device better. Katie mentioned "people." Michelle said "everything." Jon joked, "They love Jon Feucht." Everyone laughed.

But Neil took a different tact: "No regular kids here. I love that. Don't feel like an outcast," which led Katie to say, "It makes me feel normal," and Gene to say, "We are like regular people." Diane said camp makes her "feel smart." Neil added, "You feel happy here."

Sensing that it was almost time to break for lunch, Jon said, "Now it's my turn. . . . What have I learned?" Sarah said, "Nothing," and Jon retorted, "Does anyone want to take her home?" I am becoming fond of the pacing of their humor. Then Jon concluded: "I think the biggest thing is that we need hope even when hope is nowhere around. . . . There is an old saying: 'Live life through the eyes of other people to find yourself,' and this week I did that. I'm lucky to have each one of you in my life." Everyone applauded. Megan's mother, with tears in her eyes, said, "Thank you so much for starting this camp. It means a lot for all of us." Cody added, "Thank you. I feel the same." Other campers said: "Thank you." "Thanks." "Thank you, Jon." I felt happy for Jon, hoping his doubts about continuing with AVA had been laid to rest. Then he said, "Rub-a-dub-dub, let's go get some grub." Everyone laughed again.

That night we did not have dinner in the regular dining hall. Quite frankly, the food had been pretty bad. The last meal of camp would be a buffet dinner held in the university center, followed by a dance. I was hoping that the food would be better; it was, but only slightly. Megan and her mother had been taking photos during the camp, and they showed us a slide show covering the entire week. Clearly the campers have had a great time. I did too.

After we ate, Jon sat in the front of the room and offered a few words of appreciation for Dan and Lauren. Dan said he thought they had only "touched the surface" of what AVA could become. This pleased Jon a great deal. He needs to be striving toward a goal and now feels there is more to be accomplished. Then Jon, Dan, and Lauren took turns calling up each camper, one by one, giving them a certificate of appreciation and saying a few words about the positive attributes of each one of them. It really was a touching scene, and I thought that it has been a privilege for me to get to know these young people and their families. Just a few days ago they were strangers to me, a group of people with disabilities but not individual people. Now I saw them as distinct personalities. I will miss them, but hope to see them again. In the meantime, Jon and I have developed a closer relationship and that is gratifying, too.

For the dance, AVA had hired a professional DJ. I looked on as some of the campers danced in their wheelchairs. Dahlia bounced off her seat as she maneuvered her power chair around the floor. Other campers were given physical support by their parents or attendants. Cody and Neil were strapped into their walkers, which I hadn't seen up to now, wheeling about the floor in free-floating motion. I thought about how liberating it must feel for them to be able to be themselves, among others who are like them and who care about them, to enjoy a dance without the scrutinizing and sometimes hostile gaze from what Neil calls "regular" people. I wondered if it is possible to not notice their disabilities. At first I thought, not entirely, because our brains are hard-wired to scan our environment and notice differences from the routine or "expected average" (Miller and Sammons 1999:7). But through habitua-tion to new experiences it is possible to become more nonchalant or even appreciative of such differences.

During my time at the camp and subsequent visits to Jon's home, I be-came more acclimated to viewing the intercorporeality of the exchange be-tween caregivers and the cared-for as a natural part of human interaction. Gail Weiss observes that the "experience of being embodied is never a pri-vate affair," and we are continually defined in terms of our intercorporeality with others (1999:4). John Killacky (2004) adds that our connectivity to the world is deepened not diminished by our dependency on others. This is a dimension of the human experience that I think is missing from feminist critiques of care-giving as exploitative unpaid or underpaid labor (Glenn 2010; Kittay and Kittay 2002; Meyer 2000). I do not wish to negate the veracity of these critiques; I would be naïve to do so. But I do want to suggest that the care that is given to disabled youths like the AVA campers is not a wholly onerous burden on the caregivers, for there are, in Sarah Smith Rainey's (2011) terms, considerable "pleasures of care." To be sure, the parental caregivers I witnessed at the camp are often exhausted and in need of more support, both financial and otherwise. But their loving "work" is rewarding and rewarded as well. As Rainey observes, care-giving at its best entails a "mutually reinforcing connection" whereby those being cared for reciprocate "in a variety of ways, including direct response ('thank you'), personal delight ('Oh, that feels so much better'), and growth (care allows the cared-for's pursuit of happiness)" (2011:13–14; see also Noddings 1984).

Lastly, it is worth noting that in retrospect I realized that during my five days at camp I had not given much thought to the fact that Dan uses a wheelchair. There is really very little about his disability that prevents Dan, with appropriate accessibility accommodations, from doing whatever he chooses to do; and I was reminded of Jon's earlier remark about Melvin Juette, when he said that he didn't even think Melvin, who uses a manual wheelchair for mobility and who has no physical impairment above his hips, was even disabled (see Chapter 1). Be that as it may, I look forward to a day when the campers, with the aid of their AAC devices and whatever caregiving they need to live independently, will be able to reach their dreams too. Maybe then we will no longer view them as "really disabled" at all. Rather, like I view Jon, we would see them as intelligent, humorous, and determined, or whatever affirmative characteristics best describe their individuality as human beings.

NOTES

1. For further consideration of phenomenology in the context of disability studies, see also Papadimitriou (2008b); Papadimitriou and Stone (2011); Turner (2001).

2. This ethnographic account is adapted from Berger and Feucht (2012).

3. Except for Dan Price, Lauren Zubow, and Sarah Feucht, all staff, campers, and parents are referred to with pseudonyms.

4. See chapter 2, note 9.

5. See chapter 2, note 5.

6. For a discussion of these policies in the context of qualitative inquiry, see Denzin and Giardina (2012).

7. For a critique of the *Wicked* musical from a critical disability studies perspective, see Rainey (2011).

8. The song Peter played was not the same as the similarly titled religious song that I found on the Web.

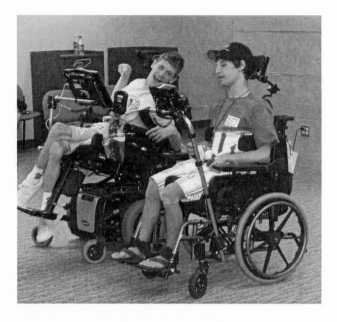

Mike Hipple (left) and Chris Sawka (right) volunteer as peer mentors at the AVA camp (2013). Permission by Mike Hipple and Chris Sawka.

Gregory Nelson (2013). Permission by Gregory Nelson.

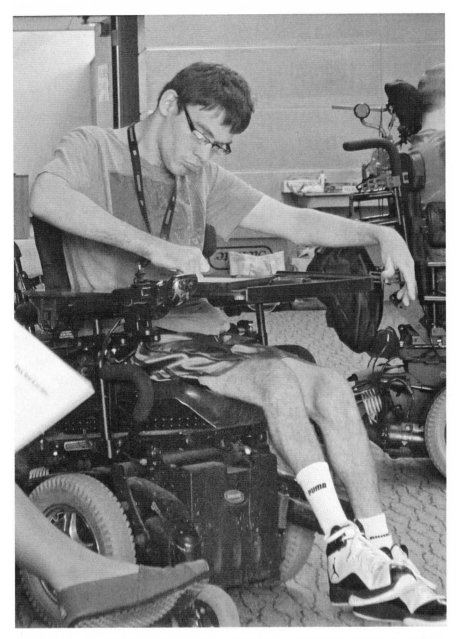

Brock Davis, the fastest communicator at the camp, volunteers as a peer mentor (2013). Permission by Brock Davis.

Maria Braun (2013). Permission by Maria Braun.

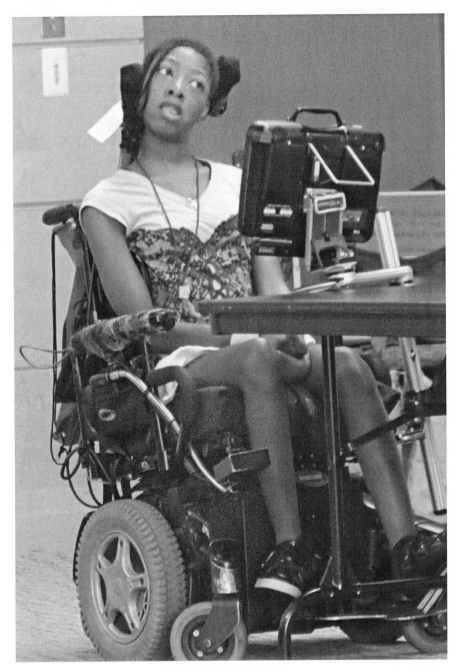

Antrice Bailey (2013). Permission by Antrice Bailey.

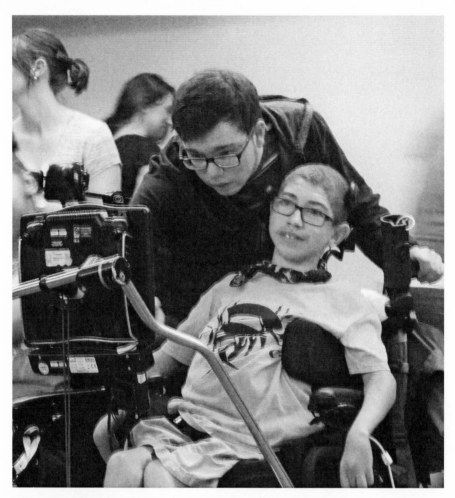

Nolan Thornton with friend/caregiver Wesley Rice (2013). Permission by Nolan Thornton and Wesley Rice.

Deena Giriyappa with teacher/caregiver Laura Zeimer (2013). Permission by Deena Giriyappa and Laura Zeimer.

Chapter Six

Travels with Jon and Sarah: A Journey through Space and Time

As part of the evolving process of our collaboration, Ron submitted an article based on his ethnography of the 2011 AVA camp to *Qualitative Inquiry*, a journal edited by Norman Denzin (Berger and Feucht 2012). Norman accepted the article for publication and subsequently invited Ron to organize a session on disability at the International Congress of Qualitative Inquiry (ICQI) held at the University of Illinois at Urbana-Champaign (U of I) in May 2012. Together with Jennifer, we decided to call the session "Disability and Qualitative Inquiry: Rethinking an Ableist World." Our idea was to feature Jon "performing" use of his communication device to enact a simulation of the 2011 summer camp and give the audience a sense of what it is like to speak and hear through augmentative communication; and we invited two other colleagues/friends who are also doing work on disability, Carla Corroto and Marjorie DeVault, to help us round out the 80–minute session.

The experience we describe in this chapter, a journey through time and space that occurred over a period of four days, is another instance of phenomenological seeing that utilizes participant observation research to illuminate the lived experience of disability, as the trip afforded the opportunity for Ron to observe Jon in a variety of circumstances and social milieus. As with the previous chapter, this relational ethnography is narrated in Ron's voice as a temporally unfolding experience. [1]

DAY ONE

When Jon first committed to going to the ICQI, we anticipated that he would travel separately in his own vehicle, accompanied by his father, who would drive their family van that can hold Jon's power wheelchair. Because of his physical impairment, Jon cannot feed himself on his own and requires the assistance of a family member or paid personal assistant. He expected his father to handle this responsibility during the excursion to Urbana-Champaign.

As we approached the date of the Congress, Jon's father said he was unable to make the trip, and in his place, Jon asked if I would be comfortable driving the van and traveling together. His wife Sarah would accompany us and help him with his daily needs. Although Sarah, who also has cerebral palsy, uses a power scooter for mobility and a computerized device to speak, unlike Jon she has nearly full use of her upper body, which enables her to assist him when necessary.

I was a little apprehensive about this alternative plan, unsure not only about driving the van but also about what else it would entail; and I wondered what it would mean for my flexibility to do as I wish at the Congress. But this was the only way Jon was able to attend.

On the day of our departure, I arrived at Jon and Sarah's home in Whitewater, Wisconsin, on Wednesday afternoon and was greeted in their open garage by Sarah. The van was parked in the garage, and I asked Sarah if the keys were in the vehicle so I could move it into the driveway to prepare it for loading their luggage, which was already in the garage, and their wheelchairs. Sarah nodded yes and I proceeded to move the van. Jon then came out of the house with his caretaker Danielle. I opened the rear doors of the van and saw the power lift that had to be lowered to get the wheelchairs inside. I did not know how to use it and fumbled with the equipment. Conceding I needed help, Sarah showed me what to do.

I was not sure what their plans were for seating. Would they both sit in their wheelchairs, or would they transfer to the seat? Sarah positioned her chair on the lift and got into the van. I asked her if she planned to transfer into the backseat, and she nodded yes. Now I wondered about Jon. Apparently he wanted to sit in the front seat. Helping Jon out of his chair, Danielle held him around the chest as he walked awkwardly to the front of the van and she helped him up into the seat. This was a responsibility I would have to assume for the rest of the trip.

Next it fell upon me to load Jon's wheelchair into the van. I stood beside the chair and manipulated the joystick to get it into the lift. I had a little trouble maneuvering the chair the first few times I tried it, but I got better at it as time went on. With the chair in the van, we took off. It had been a long time since I had driven a vehicle like this, but I felt comfortable at the wheel.

Jon, sitting beside me, rode with his augmentative communication device in his lap so we could talk. Sarah, on the other hand, did not keep her device on, as I learned is typical of her. The difference between the two of them, I surmised, is that Jon always has his device accessible on a frontal tray that is attached to his chair. But Sarah uses a smaller scooter-like chair that does not have a frontal tray; and she stores her device in a basket that is attached to the rear of her chair, only pulling it out when she wants to talk. Another difference, too, is that Jon's device speaks in a man's voice, while Sarah's speaks in a woman's voice. About Sarah, I should also mention that she has a wonderful smile that can light up a room. She is not as talkative as Jon, and tends to speak in single sentences, but she has a delightful anticipatory look of enthusiasm on her face when she is typing into her device. Jon, on the other hand, is more likely to speak in multiple sentences, and since his disability is more involved than Sarah's, he has to work harder to type. For expediency, when Jon and Sarah are talking to each other, they often use hand signs, which Sarah taught to Jon, to communicate.

We were less than an hour on the road when Jon said he needed a bathroom break. I pulled into a convenience store/gas station and parked the van. I asked Jon if he wanted to use his wheelchair or if I should assist him, as did Danielle, into the bathroom in the store. He asked me, "Are you comfortable?"—suggesting that it was up to me. Knowing that I had some difficulty manipulating the chair in and out of the van, I thought (mistakenly) that it would be easier for me to help Jon.

Before we began, I went into the store to scout out the location of the bathroom, casually informing the clerk that we would be coming in. Then I returned to the van and helped Jon as he slid off his seat and onto the ground. Although Jon supported himself with his legs and walked on his own accord, the bulk of the leverage for carrying his 95 pound frame depended on me. I held him tightly around his chest under his armpits as we walked into the store. The clerk nodded to us with a friendly smile, while the rest of the customers did not seem to pay much attention. This, I thought, was better than the staring or peculiar looks I might have expected.

In their study of the phenomenon of staring, Michael Lenney and Howard Sercombe note that nondisabled people often feel a "conflict between the 'desire to stare' and the 'desire not to stare" at disability differences (2002:8). On the one hand, it is impolite to stare; on the other hand, it is impolite to act as if disabled people are invisible. But in the context of a convenience store, ignoring Jon's disability difference that patrons must have assuredly observed was arguably the polite thing to do. I also would not dismiss the fact that although people with disabilities are often the recipients of unpleasant reactions from others, there is still much kindness in the world (Cahill and Eggleston 1995).

As we entered the bathroom, I was not sure what would happen next. Jon motioned that we needed to move into the bathroom stall. I continued to hold him as he pulled down his pants and urinated. When we returned to the car, I asked Jon for some feedback on how best to help him. "I was turning red," he typed into his device, indicating that I had been holding him too tight. My back was hurting me, too. Next time, I thought, we will use the wheelchair.

As we continued on our way, Jon started typing on his keyboard. Although Jon is a proficient user of his device, it can take a while for him to complete his thoughts. Having already spent a good deal of time with Jon, I was acclimated to the slow pace of our conversational exchange. In fact, on a long trip—our journey took about 4 ½ hours—it nicely filled up the time and I rarely turned up the radio to fill in patches of silence. At the same time, I wondered how others at the Congress would react, because timing in conversational exchanges is an issue that augmentative communication users often face with nondisabled speakers who don't have the patience to wait for them to complete their thoughts. Often people feel inclined to fill in the gaps and complete sentences before the user has a chance to finish (Hodge 2007).

About halfway through our trip, we decided to stop at a McDonald's restaurant for a break. We unloaded the two wheelchairs, entered the building, and approached the counter. Jon has several food allergies and asked the young woman behind the counter if they use milk products in their smoothies. She said it had yogurt, and he ordered an iced drink instead. As Sarah and I placed our orders, Jon went into the bathroom on his own accord. When he returned, he asked me to empty the juice from his drink bottle attached to his wheelchair and fill it with his iced drink. After some fumbling with the bottle, I saw that Jon is able to drink on his own.

Back on the road, Jon and Sarah realized that they had forgotten to bring their food blender. One of the effects of Jon's CP is that he has trouble swallowing and can only eat soft foods. This meant that we would have to purchase one when we got to Urbana-Champaign. Upon our arrival, we looked for a department store and spotted a Kohl's. Unloading the wheelchairs once more, we went into the store. Jon said to me, "Study us." What I assumed he had in mind was to watch people's reactions. But no one seemed to pay any attention. If they were staring at Jon and Sarah, they were doing a good job of hiding it.

We went over to the home appliance section, and Sarah wasted little time picking out a small Cuisinart blender. At the check-out counter, Sarah handled the payment with her credit card as the clerk tried to make friendly chatter, saying something about how the picture of food on the box of the blender was making her hungry. Her tone seemed a tad patronizing, but I didn't want to read too much into it. Clearly she was trying to act nonchalant and friendly toward the somewhat unusual customers she was serving.

Months earlier, when I had preregistered for the Congress, Norman had invited me to reserve a room in the Illini Union Hotel, the central location of the Congress on the U of I campus. Later, Jon made his own reservation at a Red Roof Inn at a cheaper rate. Upon arriving at the Red Roof, we unloaded the wheelchairs and I sensed that Jon was a little uncomfortable about the clientele that was hanging around in the parking lot. Maybe he thought they were riff-raff, I wondered.

We proceeded to the registration desk in the hotel, where we learned that there were no first-floor vacancies and no elevators in the building (when Jon made the reservation, he did not request a first-floor room). Speaking for Jon and Sarah, I asked the clerk if he would call the nearby Holiday Inn to see if they had an opening. The clerk accommodated my request and fortunately they did. As we reloaded the wheelchairs into the van, Jon said that he was "grateful for the screw-up."

Upon arriving at the Holiday Inn, I unloaded their luggage and made sure that Jon and Sarah got checked into their room. Before I left, Jon asked if I would make a take-out "food run." He had noticed an Olive Garden and asked for chicken parmesan; Sarah ordered shrimp scampi. I left to pick up the food and returned to find the blender set up and ready to go. I asked if there was anything else they needed, and then left for the night.

DAY TWO

When I arrived at the Holiday Inn the next morning, I found Jon and Sarah eating breakfast at the restaurant that is located in the main area of the hotel. Sarah was feeding Jon pancakes drenched with syrup. Jon had food dribbled on his chin and shirt, and I resisted the urge to want to wipe him clean. It reminded me about what Jon's sister Janeen had said about him being a messy eater (see chapter 2). Jon often coughs when he eats, too, which can be a little alarming, but Sarah told me not to worry—it is how he clears his throat. When they finished eating, Sarah paid the bill and we headed off to U of I.

For the short distance we traveled today, both Jon and Sarah rode in their wheelchairs. This was a lot easier than the day before, when they had to transfer in and out of their chairs every time they got in and out of the van. The Congress did not begin until later in the day, and Jon had arranged two meetings. The first was with Mike Frogley, the wheelchair basketball coach at U of I, who has an office in the Rehabilitation Education Center on campus. Mike, who was paralyzed in a car accident when he was 21 years old, is a graduate of the University of Wisconsin-Whitewater, a former UWW wheelchair basketball player and coach, and the coordinator of the disability sports camp that Jon had attended years back (see chapter 2). Jon and Mike knew each other quite well, and it was to be a reunion of old friends. I also knew Mike because I had interviewed him for a life history study I did on UWW wheelchair basketball players (Berger 2009).

The four of us crowded into Mike's small office and chatted for about 75 minutes. Jon and Mike reminisced for a while and then Jon said he wanted to tell him something important—that he was recently diagnosed with bipolar disorder, which he had finally gotten under control with the proper medication. Up until recently, Jon added, he hadn't been properly diagnosed and had even been given medication that may have made his bipolar condition worse. Mike's reaction was that Jon's bipolar condition was just another disability— no big deal. But the point Jon wanted to make to his old friend was that he was now ready to pursue one of his life goals—earning a doctoral degree, something he had wanted to do since receiving his master's degree in special education a few years ago. Jon and I had talked about this yesterday during our drive, when I learned that one of his objectives for going to the ICQI was to explore opportunities for earning an online doctorate in special education at U of I, which is known as a leading educational institution for disability programs and services.[2] Thus Jon thought there might be some opportunities for him here. This was to be part of his agenda for our second meeting that day.

Jon, Sarah, and I said our good byes to Mike and made our way out of the building. As I walked ahead to the van parked across the street to prepare the lift, Jon and Sarah paused to read a wall plaque dedicated to Timothy Nugent, the man who founded U of I's comprehensive program for students with disabilities, the first in the United States, in 1948; he was also a major figure in the development of wheelchair basketball, a pursuit for disabled people that has been of considerable interest to me (Berger 2009). When I got to the van I found that the key would not open the door lock. I tried a few times and then turned around and saw Jon across the street waving his arms and Sarah positioned on my side of the street next to the right van, which was similar in color to the wrong one I was trying to open. But the interesting thing about this, I thought, besides the fact that I looked foolish, was that Jon and Sarah weren't able to shout out to stop me before I made my blunder. Jon said he was trying to shout "hey" in his dysarthric voice to get my attention, but I didn't hear him.[3]

With this minor mishap behind us, we headed to the Illini Union Hotel located across campus. We found a handicap parking space adjacent to the building, exited the van, and entered the front of the impressive burnt-orange brick structure with white pillars and white window trimmings through an entrance that was marked handicap accessible. The wheelchair ramp was quite narrow and jackknifed several times before you could actually get into the lobby. Jon and Sarah, especially Jon, were unable to make the turns without moving their wheelchairs back and forth at these spots. The "accessible" ramp was apparently designed for smaller manual wheelchairs, not power chairs. Later we learned there was an easier way to get in and out of the building through a side entrance.

We had a couple of hours before Jon's second appointment, and we decided to part ways for a while. Jon and Sarah went out to get something to eat and explore the local shops, and I registered for the Congress and checked out the book exhibit. Later when I met up with them, Jon was wearing an orange baseball cap and Sarah had her fingernails painted orange—orange being the U of I school color. We still had a little time before our second meeting, so I asked Jon if he would like me to show him where to register.

We approached the registration desk and stood/sat in front of the same woman who had registered me earlier. She recognized me and asked me Jon's name. This is a common experience for people with disabilities—people ask others to speak for them (Cahill and Eggleston 1995). I said to her, "Let him tell you. That's part of the fun." Later I thought that my comment about "part of the fun" was an odd thing for me to have said—even if I was having fun watching people's reactions to Jon. But her response was even more interesting, as she said "thanks" in a mildly sarcastic tone that suggested she did not have the patience for what was transpiring.

By now it was time for the second meeting Jon had arranged, this one with Jon Gunderson, coordinator of Assistive Communication and Information Technology at U of I. Jon had two topics on his mind: exploring the idea of developing a summer camp like Authentic Voices of America at U of I, and opportunities for obtaining an online doctoral degree.

We met Gunderson in the main area of the Union where they served coffee, sandwiches, and light snacks; and where people worked at their laptops or were absorbed in their smartphones. Gunderson said that two or three other university people might join us. During our 90 minute conversation with him, a couple people came and went, but Mark Hasegawa-Johnson, a professor of computer engineering, was the only one who stayed for any length of time. He said he was working on some advanced augmentative communication technology and was interested in recruiting actual users for his project. We started by talking about AVA, and on his laptop Jon showed them a short promotional video about the camp called "Unlocking the Voice Within" that is available on YouTube. Everyone watched the video with great interest, and I sensed that the idea of starting a camp like this at U of I was appealing. Gunderson said he might like to visit Jon's camp in person, but I got the impression that he was only being polite and would not follow-through on this, which he hasn't.

More interestingly, for the purpose of what it revealed about augmentative communication, this was the first time I had been in a group conversation with Jon with people who did not already know him, and I realized that the nuances of conversational exchanges in this context were more complex than talking to Jon one-on-one. Should the rest of us remain silent while Jon was typing his message? Or should we continue our conversation until he was ready to speak? Moreover, Jon's responses tended to be brief, and I found myself wanting to fill in details about AVA that he had left out.

Next, we talked a little about Hasegawa-Johnson's project, which in-volves the development of software technology with greater "context aware" word-predictive power. If a user is in a restaurant, for example, the device would be preprogrammed with a wider set of food-oriented statements that would make for faster communication. Jon, however, said he had "mixed feelings" about what Hasegawa-Johnson is doing. Apparently Jon was con-cerned about devices that take away the speaker's individualized voice, that is, devices that speak *for* the person rather than allowing the person to speak for him- or herself. Jon pointed out that being in a restaurant did not mean that the main part of a conversation was oriented toward food. "We have been sitting here and talking for an hour," Jon said, "and we have been talking about everything but food." What Jon was getting at, I thought, is that AAC users do not simply desire to communicate about mundane tasks; they also want to be able to engage in higher-level conversations about all sorts of matters that may be beyond the power of predictive technologies. Additional-ly, prerecorded messages don't always fit well into a conversational ex-change; they may contain too much or too little information or may only be partially relevant to the topic. If the user needs to edit the message, then the speed advantage of the prerecorded message is attenuated. In a study of the interactions between disabled patrons and nondisabled salesclerks, for exam-ple, Linda Hoag and colleagues found that salesclerks preferred AAC users to take "the time to deliver an entirely relevant message" rather than deliver-ing a "partly relevant message with minimal delay" (Hoag et al. 2004:1272). They also rated users more competent individuals when they took the time to communicate their responses.

Following this exchange, Jon brought up the main topic of his agenda: getting an online doctoral degree. No such program at that level existed at U of I, said Gunderson and Hasegawa-Johnson, and they acted as if this was a rather unusual request. Jon would have to talk to the people in the special education department, they told him. But they were doubtful that Jon's idea would be well received. At a minimum he would probably need to be in residence for a year or so. When Gunderson and Hasegawa-Johnson pointed out that something like this had never been done at U of I before, I suggested that there was always a first time, rhetorically adding, "Isn't U of I known for its state-of-the-art programs for students with disabilities?" Still, Jon left the meeting feeling disappointed with their reaction to his query.

It was getting late and almost time for the official opening of the ICQI. Jon and Sarah were not sure if they wanted to go or do something else. If they decided to come, I told them, I would meet them upstairs in the ball-room where the plenary session was being held.

I arrived at the session a little early and found a seat. By the time we were ready to start, the large hall was filled with a standing-room-only crowd. Norman Denzin made some welcoming remarks, noting the growth of the conference over the years, with about 1400 delegates representing 67 countries in attendance this year.[4] I looked around the ballroom but did not see Jon and Sarah. They would miss the keynote addresses by Sara Delamont (2013) and Paul Atkinson (2013). Their talks dealt with issues of performativity, narrative, and literary representation; and Delamont left us with a reminder of Erving Goffman's invocation to "go out and uncover something." That is what I have been doing, indeed.

When the plenary session was over, I went downstairs to look for Jon and Sarah. When I didn't find them, I decided to make my way to the Midwest BBQ that was being held at another part of campus. After enjoying some food and listening to the live music for a while, I returned to the Union where I found Jon and Sarah inquiring about my whereabouts at the registration desk. They appeared a little agitated, having been looking for me for about an hour. We realized we had neglected to exchange cell phone numbers and immediately entered them into our respective phones. I asked them if they wanted me to take them back to the Holiday Inn and they said yes.

Two women in the lobby who were attending the conference overheard me mention the Holiday Inn and asked if I could give them a ride. As we walked back to the van, we learned that they had come all the way from New Zealand. The younger of the two women easily flowed into conversation with Jon. Once in the van, we told them about our session the next day, and the younger one said she would try to attend (which she did).

DAY THREE

I started my day by attending a morning session on disability, one of six at the Congress, before picking up Jon and Sarah. Our session was scheduled for 1:00 p.m. and we planned to meet in the Union with Jennifer beforehand to discuss our presentation. Previously I had prepared a script to outline the summer camp simulation and the roles the three of us would play. This script included a brief prerecorded excerpt from one of Jon's "Straight Talk" speeches that he had given at the camp. But just prior to the Congress, the component of his device that allows him to play it malfunctioned. "Plan B" was to have me read the excerpt. I also asked Jon to prepare a response to a question that I would ask him at the beginning of our presentation: "What would you do if your device didn't work at the start of an actual camp?"

We planned our presentation to revolve around seven questions that Jon or Lauren Zubow, the speech pathologist who assisted him at the camp, had asked of the young campers:

> What do you think it means to be disabled? What are a couple of things you want to do in your life? Have any of you ever given up hope? Have you ever given up something you later regretted? Does anybody know what I mean by

the reverse side of success? If you get down, what do you do to lift your spirits? What are some things you love about camp?

We would ask our ICQI audience to "role-play" as campers and respond to these questions. Jennifer and I would also offer a sample of the real campers' responses; and Sarah would add responses of her own, allowing the audience to hear another actual AAC speaker.

At a prearranged time we met Jennifer in the parking lot and made our way to the side entrance of the building. With Jon and Sarah ahead of us, Jennifer asked me, "So, how was the drive?" I replied "Interesting," by which I meant to imply that we would talk more about it later. Like the front entrance, this side entrance had a zigzag structure and seemed constructed for manual wheelchairs. But it was a little wider than the front entrance and somewhat easier for Jon and Sarah to maneuver.

Later Jennifer would tell me that when she had driven up to the Illini Union Hotel, she was enamored by the beauty of the old buildings that lined the streets of this bustling college town. Jennifer loves old college buildings, with their bricks and ivy and pillars; she just loves the "feel" of those spaces. But witnessing Jon and Sarah traverse the rather unwelcoming side entrance made her acutely aware of the way in which the architecture made their experience of this old building so much different from hers.

We headed to the café area and positioned ourselves around a table. While Jennifer and I talked, Jon typed and stored the seven questions I had prepared into his device as rapidly as he could; these he would be able to play back during our session. While he was doing this, he was not participating in our conversation, and neither was Sarah. When I left to get some food, Jennifer later told me, she tried to engage Sarah in a one-on-one conversation, asking her, "What was it like driving down with Ron?" Sarah laughed and set about answering. Unlike Jon, who usually allows his words to come out one at a time as he speaks, Sarah waits until she has completed her input before playing her comment out loud. As Jennifer waited anxiously to hear her response, Jon looked up and exchanged some signs and gestures with Sarah about the question Jennifer had asked. But by the time Sarah was ready to play her response, I had returned, and not knowing that Sarah was about to speak, interrupted the silence by starting to talk about other matters. Sarah never played her response, nor did Jennifer ask her to do so. In retrospect, we all wish we had been more open about the dilemmas of communicating in a group situation, so we could have talked about how we wanted to converse.

What also struck Jennifer about this incident, which she later shared with me, was that the silence, the "white pages" of the interaction if you will (Clandinin 2013), was actually part of the conversation, though the conversation did not take the shape of the expected back and forth. Moreover, the brief moment Jennifer had with me earlier, when she asked me about the trip with Jon and Sarah in privacy, could not happen in the same way. The potential rapport with Sarah that Jennifer might have been able to build by asking her question, a secret between Sarah and Jennifer about how Sarah felt about spending several hours in a car with a man (me) she barely knew, did not work, because they did not have the time or space to do it.

As Jon finished his typing, he said he needed to use the bathroom, and he asked me if I knew where it was. I pointed in the direction behind me, and Jon asked, "Accessible?" Frankly I didn't know, which was an uncertainty that introduced another moment where we were all unclear about how to proceed. I suggested that Jon could go and ask someone, or, he could go and "scout it out" himself. It seemed that we all didn't know what the appropriate action should be. This puzzlement over whether this public building had an accessible bathroom was another instance of Jon's experience of this building as so much different from Jennifer's and mine. With the grandeur of old universities, especially this one, nondisabled people tend to see the big heavy wooden doors and old-fashioned elevators as quaint and historic. But for Jon, the main element of the experience revolved around the question of access and whether he was really "welcome here"—an element that now became a concern for us all. After some deliberation and confusion about the appropriate thing to do, Jon left to figure it out for himself.

While Jon was gone, Jennifer and I discussed some issues about an article we were writing on medical decision-making that was peripheral to our work with Jon, and I asked her to write something about her experience with her father's illness (Berger et al. 2013). All the while, Sarah sat quietly as we talked. At one point I apologized to Sarah about the "shop talk," but she said she wasn't listening to what we were saying.

When Jon returned, Jennifer was talking about how her father was forced by his insurance company to take on a "hospice status" even though he had not wanted to do so. Jon wanted to tell us about a similar experience with an insurance company that had happened to him. At this point, the fast-paced conversation Jennifer and I were having slowed, as we listened to Jon tell a personal story about his own involvement with a healthcare facility where he had been hospitalized. This story took some 10 minutes for him to tell, during which time other things were going on at the table. I was trying to peel an orange and was having trouble doing so. Sarah was laughing at me, as Jon continued to type and talk, one word at a time. Later Jennifer told me that at first she thought these distractions could be interpreted as rude to Jon; he was, after all, not shooting the breeze, but talking about a rather serious experience. But then, she thought, this could be happening in any situation, when multiple things are going on as people talk/text/type or simply look around while someone is trying to say something. Still, there was a difference in how our conversation proceeded, because when Jon was finished, the conversation ended abruptly, with no one really commenting on what he had said. In the conference atmosphere that Jennifer and I are used to, this sharing of experience, or sharing of information corresponding to another's work, might be treated as a window of opportunity for future deliberation, even collaboration. Instead, due in part to the nature of Jon's mode of communication and the time it took him to contribute and be part of the temporal social space we are occupying, it seemed as if his story was treated almost lightheartedly and then dismissed without comment. Part of the problem, however, was by the time Jon had finished his remarks, we were ready to move on to the room of our presentation.

Before we left the café, Sarah said she needed a bathroom break, too. Meanwhile, I had run into some other people I knew and was making plans for dinner, and then said I was going to head up to the room and for the others to meet me there. I pointed in the direction of the elevators and asked Jennifer if she would accompany Jon and Sarah to the room.

Once I left, Jennifer later told me, she had some time alone with Jon and again asked about driving to U of I with me. He joked about the incident when I had tried to get into the wrong van, but then said that he now "questions the Ph.D." By the time he had said this, Sarah was back and it was getting late, so Jennifer didn't ask anything else.

The three of them headed for the elevators and found that this majestic building only had old, small elevator cars. There was no way that they could all get into one, let alone anyone else, and there was a line to get on. There also was some confusion as people held the elevator door open for them, but they decided to wait for the next elevator.

When the next elevator arrived, already partially filled, Sarah and Jennifer got on but there was no room for Jon. Jennifer asked Jon, "Can you get the next one? Go to the fourth floor." But there was no time for Jon to respond before the doors closed and they took off.

Jennifer later told me that Sarah was visibly nervous, and when they got off on the fourth floor, they were unsure if they were in the right place. Several elevators came but there was no Jon. When they found me, Jennifer asked, "Should I go get Jon?" Sarah nodded a vigorous YES and Jennifer went down, not sure if she and Jon would miss each other as Jon came up and she went down. But Jon was still on the ground floor. Without saying anything about what had transpired, they got onto the elevator together and went up to the fourth floor.

When we all finally arrived at our session room, it was incredibly small, with a slanted ceiling that made us feel as if we were packed like sardines in a can. The audience chairs were positioned in rows, with about four on each side of a narrow aisle. At the front of the room was a table with space for two people and a large screen that had been pulled down from a previous session. I asked Jon to come up to the front of the room, but there was little space for him to turn his chair around, and when he did he "banged" into the screen, startling everyone in the room. Jennifer and I sat down behind the table, while I asked Carla Corroto and Marjorie DeVault, who were also part of our session, to sit in the front row and come up to the front when it was time to make their presentations.

The time for our session was about to begin. Our plan was for Carla and Marjorie to speak for 15 minutes apiece, and for Jon, Jennifer, and me to take about 30 minutes, leaving the rest of the time for questions and discussion with the audience. All told, about a dozen people attended all or part of the session—some came in late and some left early—with a minimum of eight people present at any one time.

After Carla and Marjorie finished their presentations—Carla spoke about the teaching of universal design in architecture schools, and Marjorie about the challenges Deaf people face in the healthcare system—we began the summer camp simulation. I set things up, noting the need for "Plan B" because of Jon's malfunctioning equipment. I asked Jon what he would do if his equipment was not working at the time of the actual camp. He said, "I would change my name to Juan and move to Mexico so nobody could blame me for a bad camp." This touch of humor set a nice tone for the presentation, giving the audience a sense of Jon's personality and creating a comfortable atmosphere. Indeed, previous studies find that humor is a good way to ease people's discomfort with disability (Cahill and Eggleston 1994, 1995).

As we had arranged, Jennifer started things off with some remarks about our project and methodological process to set up the simulation of the camp (see chapter 1). Then I cued Jon to start asking the audience questions, hoping to elicit their participation. Insofar as Jon typed the questions into his device rather hastily, the verbal output contained some mistakes and I felt the need to clarify what he was asking. I didn't think much about this at the time, but later Jennifer said she wondered how Jon felt about it. He told us that he used to be a perfectionist but now accepts the fact that he will make mistakes and that everyone has times when they stumble over their words.

The first few questions were met with silence, and Jennifer and I filled in the gaps by reproducing the actual responses the youths had given at the camp. But after a while the audience got into it and started participating, leading to a successful simulation of the camp. The nature of the session took a different turn during the question-and-answer period, however. When Jon responded to questions and made statements in "real time," not relying on his prerecorded input, the true performative objective of our presentation began to unfold. Now the audience was expected to wait in silence for Jon to input his thoughts. Periods of silence can be awkward in interpersonal encounters, especially in a professional setting like this. But this was/is the only way to convey the lived experience of AAC. The audience's patience for this period of silence required a suspension of ableist expectations about conversational exchanges. Without such patience, AAC users will never be fully integrated into the mainstream of interpersonal communicative discourse.

While I calmly waited for the interaction to unfold, Jennifer was a little nervous as the room filled with silence amidst fidgeting and low murmurs as Jon typed out his embellished responses, one letter at a time. When one woman asked a question that Jon could have answered with an abbreviated "yes" or "no," he wanted to elaborate. As he made a gesture indicating he wanted to follow-up his initial "yes" response, the woman who asked the question quickly said, "So the short answer is yes," as if perhaps to say, you don't need to say any more. We were not sure if this woman's intent was to give Jon the *option* of not giving a longer response, or if she wanted to spare herself and the rest of the audience the inevitable silence that was about to ensue, but what struck us most about this moment, is that in continuing Jon was asserting his right to be heard.

In Jennifer's and my experience, the social organization of time in the temporal-spatial milieu of a professional conference always creates a feeling of constraint. More often than not, in order to accommodate as many present-ers as possible, the typical time slot granted for presentations creates a cli-mate in which participants feel rushed to complete their remarks, and ques-tions are reserved for a brief and sometimes perfunctory time at the end. Although one of the ostensible purposes of professional conferences is to allow presenters to share their work and receive quality feedback from oth-ers—otherwise one could simply e-mail their papers to interested col-leagues—there is rarely enough time allocated for meaningful dialogue. At times the whole conference experience seems designed more for presenters to add a line to their curriculum vitas, to simply meet old friends, or if the conference is held in a desirable location, to give them a brief but paid vacation from their normal responsibilities.

In our case, however, we had planned for this constraint and allocated enough time, and in many respects the changed pace of Jon's presentation was a welcome respite from the normal pace of conference sessions. And our audience, a self-selected group that was interested in disability issues, waited patiently and respectfully for Jon to complete his remarks. Indeed, the tem-poral space that the audience granted Jon gave them the time to look at each other and exchange a few words. At first glance one might think that these low murmurs were rude, but after further consideration, we noticed this led to an even friendlier and more engaged discussion, especially as Jon re-sponded with humor and ease. Moreover, the audience was careful to ask an equal amount of questions of Carla and Marjorie—and Jon asked a question of Carla, too—so as to create a truly integrated atmosphere. When the ses-sion was over, several people went up to Jon and thanked him. Some thanked Jennifer and me as well. We all left gratified that our session had been a success.

Jennifer had to depart to take care of her infant son,[5] and Jon, Sarah, and I had a few hours to spare before dinner. Jon and Sarah were hungry, and we decided to go downstairs to the food court to get a bite to eat. Sarah ordered food for Jon and herself at the Chick-fil-A Express. She pointed to the blender that was in the basket attached to her chair, suggesting that I pull it out. I looked for a nearby wall socket and plugged it in. Sarah dropped in Jon's chicken sandwich to prepare it for Jon to eat. When he was finished eating, I offered to wash out the blender in a bathroom sink.

Before going upstairs, Jon spotted some pinball machines in the bowling alley that is adjacent to the food court, and he and Sarah played a few games. Then we split up for a while, planning to meet later at 6:00 p.m. to have dinner with Carla and Marlynn May, an old colleague/friend of mine from Wisconsin, now living in Texas, who was attending the ICQI. I had made dinner plans with Marlynn before I was certain the others would be joining us, so when he arrived, this was the first time he had met Jon and Sarah and learned of my professional collaboration with Jon. But Marlynn took everything in stride as I told him he could be part of our dinner ethnography.

We exited the Union and walked down the street to find a restaurant, eventually deciding on a small Chinese restaurant called the Evo Café. We were seated by a Chinese waiter in an isolated corner of the restaurant located in the rear. I didn't think this placement was intended to separate us from the other customers, although the thought initially crossed my mind; rather it appeared to be the only part of the restaurant that could accommodate five people and two power wheelchairs. In addition to the waiter, two other Chinese kitchen workers lingered nearby to observe us. I thought that we must have seemed like a curious group to them, but their looks were benign, even kindly. The restaurant staff did not appear to be native to the United States, and later Carla described the scene as "outsiders watching outsiders."

We ordered our food as separate dishes, rather than in group style, and when the food arrived we looked around for a wall socket for Jon's blender. Marlynn saw one next to him and offered to blend Jon's food. I was rather impressed by how nonchalantly Marlynn volunteered and performed this task, because I doubt he had ever been with or even seen an adult using a blender to prepare food in a public place. As Marlynn blended the food, the restaurant staff continued to watch us with the same kindly stares; I don't think they had ever seen anything like this either. Jon was a little self-conscious, however, because he warned us that it takes him a long time to eat.

While Jon and Sarah were focusing on their food—with Sarah alternately feeding both Jon and herself—Carla, Marlynn, and I "shop talked" about qualitative methods, and more specifically about how to address an organizational dilemma on a co-authored paper Carla and I were working on at the time (Berger et al. 2013). As we were talking, I looked over to Jon and saw that he wanted to say something. My inclination was to take the beginning of Jon's typed input, rather than his audio output, as the beginning of his entrance into our conversation, and I suggested pausing the conversation with Carla and Marlynn to wait for Jon to complete his thoughts. Earlier I noted that the nuances of a conversational exchange with Jon in a group context were more complex than talking to him one-on-one. But what was the proper protocol for the situation we found ourselves in? It is of course common in any group setting at a restaurant for people to pair off and talk separately, but in this case Jon wanted to join the conversation. Was it acceptable for the three of us to continue talking until Jon was ready to speak? Or was it more appropriate for us to patiently wait in silence, as we decided to do, while he was preparing his remarks? Not knowing the answer to these questions, I later asked Jon about it; and he said there can be no standard protocol for a situation like this because every person with a disability will prefer something different. Later Carla also admitted that she had been feeling a little bored by having to wait for Jon, although she said she often gets bored when having dinner with a group of people she has just met. At the same time, she said she felt guilty for feeling that way. To this admission, Jon observed, "Feelings are feelings and nobody should feel guilty about them," adding that it is "not always innate to be comfortable with somebody who is different from you."

These issues aside, Jon took a different meaning away from our conversation. When we finally got to hear his response, he offered a solution to the organizational dilemma we had been discussing. It was an idea that had occurred to me before, but I had not yet latched on to it and kept it front and center in my mind. Upon hearing Jon articulate the same solution, it occurred to me that he was right. "See Jon," I told him, "You are Ph.D. material." In fact, Jon said he felt a little intimidated engaging with three professors on a conceptual matter. But finding that he could hold his own gave him more confidence in his own abilities. In some ways, Jon later told me, my comment was an epiphany for him, as it brought back memories of when his physical therapist Audrey Rodar first told his parents that he was college material (see chapter 2).

As we walked back to the Union, Jon was in a reflective mood. We lagged behind the others as we stopped to talk. Two nondisabled talkers can walk and talk at the same time, but Jon has to stop when he wants to say something. "I was robbed of 20 years of my life," he said, "because of that darn bipolar." Now he could "finally move forward with the rest of my life."

As we approached the edge of campus, Jon asked me to stop. "Look up, what do you see?" he asked. "A beautiful building with a steeple," I said. Jon was pointing to the majestic Altgeld Hall, first completed in 1897, with additions in 1914, 1919, 1926, and 1956, described in the U of I *Visitor's*

Guide I had picked up in the Union as "one of the finest examples of Richardsonian Romanesque architecture in Illinois." "Beautiful," Jon said. "Do you know what the problem is with the world today? People pass that [building] billions of times and they don't understand how beautiful it is. There is no regard anymore for things like that."

DAY FOUR

On the final morning of the ICQI, it was fitting that I concluded my time at the ICQI by attending the plenary session on "Dilemmas and Challenges of Narrative Practice and Narrative Inquiry" moderated by Carolyn Ellis. I managed to get a seat in the room that filled to capacity, with people sitting on the floor and standing by the walls. Those in attendance had come to hear what some of the "heavy hitters" of the Congress, Norman Denzin among them, had to say about the state of narrative in qualitative scholarship. For the most part, with the exception of Norman's "two-act play" warning against complacency in the pursuit of the "narrative turn," the session was more *about* narrative than *of* narrative, but the discussion of the relationship between the researcher and the researched brought to mind some of the methodological issues at stake in Jennifer's and my work with Jon (see chapter 1). As I was listening, I found myself in agreement with Arthur Bochner, one of the speakers at today's session, who alluded to what he once wrote: "We can call on stories to make theoretical abstractions, or we can hear stories as a call to be vigilant to the cross-currents of life's contingencies" (2001:132). For Bochner, stories were "a means for being with others" (p. 142), and citing Arthur Frank (1995), he noted the importance of thinking *with* stories rather than *about* stories, and in doing so, making others' stories our own, by relating them to our own lives.

With these musings in mind, the session on narrative came to an end and it was time for us to leave the ICQI and head back to Wisconsin. Our ride home was uneventful. We stopped at an Arby's drive-through to get something to eat, and had a laugh as Jon told me he goes through such venues in his power wheelchair. Jon and I reflected on the past few days, but what was foremost on his mind was the matter of the online doctoral degree. Having been disappointed at the dim prospects of pursuing this degree at U of I, he was determined to investigate possibilities elsewhere. A few months later, I was pleased to learn that Jon was accepted into an online program in educational leadership and public policy at East Tennessee State University. With this he will be taking on additional time-consuming obligations, and it seems that it is time to achieve closure on this book as he moves on to the next stage of his life. Perhaps one day we will write an epilogue.

NOTES

1. This chapter, absent Jennifer's observations, is adapted from Berger and Feucht (2013).

2. A U of I *Visitor Guide* I later picked up at the Illini Union touts the university's credentials in this area: "#1 Rated as one of the most 'disability friendly' U.S. campuses. First to provide students with disabilities access to all university services, curricula, and facilities; developed first architectural accessibility standards; designed and instituted a wheelchair-accessible bus system; first to offer comprehensive wheelchair sports programming. Developed the first transitional living program for students with physical disabilities needing personal assistant support services."

3. Jon can make utterances that are intelligible in context to those who know him well, but are unintelligible to most others.

4. In 2013 the number of participants had increased to 1900.

5. Jennifer was unable to spend the rest of the day with us because she needed to nurse her infant son. Later she admitted that at times she felt that her experience as a professional woman with a child was similar to the experiences of people with disabilities. When she became pregnant with her son, her first child, she noticed how difficult it was for her to carry a bag at the airport (to avoid the check-in baggage fee) when she was traveling to visit her mother, and to have to walk up a flight of stairs or search for an out-of-the-way elevator. She felt unwelcomed at the airport, as if she was implicitly being told, "Maybe you shouldn't be flying while you're pregnant." Once her son was born, just a few months before the ICQI, her body was tied to him, needing to be physically available every one to two hours to nurse him. Just as Jon could not have attended the ICQI without Ron and Sarah's assistance, she could not have attended if her husband had been unable to travel with her. And there were no childcare accommodations at the conference that would have helped mitigate this situation. After the conference she felt, can I really do this again? But if she were to decide to not go and just stay at home, she would lose out on professional opportunities to advance her career.

Conclusion

Chapter Seven

Disability, Multiculturalism, and the American Dream

Looking back on the journey of our research project and the writing of this book, we are grateful for how much we have learned from our association. When Jon first approached Ron about writing a book about someone who is "really disabled," and when Jennifer first joined the project, little did we know what the experience would actually entail. Little did we know how much the experience would bring home the meaning of Robert McRuer's (2006, 2010) crip theory, the observation that the more significantly disabled have an epistemological stance that is capable of offering a more thoroughly penetrating critique of the often invisible, taken-for-granted social structure of ableism. We hope, too, that our readers will have come to appreciate that Jon's story, like the stories of others like him, is an experience of disability that resists reading it as tragic or pitiable. As such, in Arthur Frank's terms, Jon's story becomes a story of a *dyadic* or *communicative* body, a body that teaches by being "a body *for* other bodies," that reframes what appears to be lacking as something replete with possibility, and that turns fate and contingency into agency and self-determination and reflects "confidence in what is waiting to emerge" (1995:37, 171).

Insofar as Jon is also pleased with our efforts, with both the process of our collaboration and the results of our work, we have realized our goal of advancing the enterprise that disability studies calls emancipatory research and we call methodological empowerment (Flad, Berger, and Feucht 2011). We prefer the latter term because it is a concept that avoids the connotation of research undertaken in the context of political action by or on behalf of people with disabilities. Rather, like Amy Petersen (2011), we believe that the very act of telling one's story can be empowering in and of itself. Indeed, Jon has told us that the writing of this book has in fact changed his life. The self-reflection it entailed has led him to a greater appreciation of his parents; and it was profoundly moving for him to hear his mother say in an interview with us that he was a "lovable child." It had a direct connection, he believes, to his desire to get his life in order, "once and for all," and to the epiphany of getting diagnosed and properly treated for his bipolar condition. It gave him the confidence to put aside his self-doubts and remain steadfast about continuing with Authentic Voices of America, as well as the confidence to not rest on his laurels but to pursue his dream of earning a doctoral degree.

SUMMING UP: JON'S STORY IN SOCIAL CONTEXT

One of our goals for this book, as we indicated at the outset, has been to situate Jon's story in broader context by understanding disability not just as an individual experience but as a social phenomenon. As such, we would be remiss if we did not underscore the disability rights movement as a central element of Jon's story, a social context that is always there, always hovering in the background, the "elephant in the room" so to speak. It is this context that makes Jon's story possible, and he knows this very well. Recall his observation about Karen, a severely disabled woman he met at an AAC conference, who was a disability rights activist (chapter 3). Jon says he is glad he has not had to fight for everything he has gained as a result of this movement; and he acknowledges his ongoing contribution to the movement when he says that he views himself as someone who wants "to make people's *minds* rather than *buildings* accessible."

At the same time, it is arguably true that the disability rights movement is not the *sine qua non* of Jon's story, at least as he wants to tell it. This is a point that came up early in our research when he described two kinds of college students: those who tend to stay at home and do not "get off their behinds," and those who are advocates for themselves and actively engage their community in an effort "to make their mark on the world." Jon has little patience for a social analysis that makes excuses for the former group of students in terms of the obstacles posed by either their physical impairments or any social barriers they may face, and in doing so he chooses to privilege personal agency over social structure in his view of the world (chapter 1).

Be that as it may, we said at the outset that we did not want to characterize Jon as some sort of "supercrip," as someone whose inspirational story of courage, dedication, and hard work proves that it is possible to defy the odds and accomplish the impossible. It is not that we are opposed to readers finding Jon's story inspirational, but we do not want them to think that Jon or anyone else is a "self-made man" who can make it on their own. Indeed, without the disability rights movement there would not be a Jon Feucht as we know him today. It is in this sense that we observed that agentive action is not simply *constrained* by social structure but also *enabled* by it (chapter 1).

In their study of disability rights, however, David Engel and Frank Munger (2003) found that positive *family relationships* were typically more important than *legal rights* in the life outcomes of the people with disabilities they interviewed. More generally, Viktor Gecas (1989) observes that family relationships are typically the key factor in most individual's development of self-efficacy (if they develop it at all), that is, a person's ability to act upon rather than merely react to their external environment. In Jon's case, whatever self-efficacy or agentive capacity he has exhibited is not a trait he has acquired on his own. He would be the first to admit that his work ethic and drive to succeed were acquired from his parents. Importantly, if it had not been for the undying support of his parents, who provided him with the love, financial security, and home care he needed (assisted by his sister Janeen), he would not be the man he is today. And if his parents had not been able to navigate the educational system to find him the best accessible schools to attend, he would not have developed the intellectual tools that have enabled him to go on to college, and now pursue a doctoral degree. Although his parents were hesitant to let him go off to college to live on his own, they did not stop him from doing so, and they were able to finance his education without Jon having to go into debt by taking out student loans. After Jon graduated, they also were able to purchase an accessible house for Sarah and him to live in that they could not have otherwise afforded.

In Jon's life, there also was the University of Wisconsin-Whitewater, an accessible campus with an official institutional mission to serve students with disabilities. It is there that he was introduced to a support network of professionals who became his close friends, including Connie Wiersma of Disabled Student Services, who introduced him to an advanced speech-generating device, and Dr. Richard Lee, Dean of the Graduate School, who gave Jon a lot of personal encouragement and who allocated institutional resources for the development and growth of Authentic Voices of America. In many ways, Jon's association with Ron and Jennifer and the writing of this book is another instance of UWW opening up opportunities for him.

In these ways, the personal qualities that Jon possesses may be understood as structurally-formed capacities that are not entirely of his own making. As Abraham Maslow (1954) would remind us, the means of becoming a self-actualized person begin with the satisfaction of lower-level basic needs, needs that people with disabilities cannot take for granted, such as whether their home care assistant will arrive on time (or at all) to help them eat and bathe and get ready for the day. And Jon, too, recognizes that personal drive and ambition may not be enough. Recall Ron's conversation with Jerry at the AVA camp, who wondered whether sending his son to college would be financially worthwhile given the challenges Craig would inevitably face trying to obtain employment following graduation (chapter 5). We noted, too, that even Jon has doubts about whether he is deceiving the campers about what the future holds for them: "I say push yourself, make success work, go to college. But for what? The government doesn't want people with disabilities actually working . . . [at least] not at a middle-class level."

Although Jon blames the government for putting income caps on people who are dependent on government assistance, there is a broader structural issue that is implicated here: the ability of significantly disabled people to obtain employment in a capitalist economy that demands high productivity from workers. Mike Oliver (1990) observes that the social status of people with disabilities is largely defined by their ability or inability to perform productive labor, whereby being able-bodied means one is capable of the physical and cognitive activities expected in a particular system of labor. But in the United States, the full- or part-time employment rate for people with disabilities is less than 40 percent of the rate of the general population, and about 30 percent of disabled Americans live in poverty (Cornell University 2013; Pincus 2011; Stodden and Dowrick 2000). Engel and Munger add that in our culture "the very fact of being employed in itself confers moral citizenship . . . [and] those who do not or cannot work are typically viewed as persons who are not entitled" to the respect that is due to other adult citizens (2003:116).

Notwithstanding Jon's personal grit and determination, it is here that his class position has given him a significant advantage over so many others with his degree of disability, because without the financial support of his parents, it is not clear he would be as successful as he is today. Even AVA, which is a source of income for Jon that he uses to supplement his disability insurance, derives largely from charitable donations and fund-raising events that are organized by his relatives. For others less privileged than Jon, acknowledging this economic context is central to what Dana Lee Baker (2011) calls the "care agenda" of the disability rights movement: the need to provide funding for quality services to those who are unable to perform functional activities without assistance, including the services they need to live independently.

At the same time, as we have noted, Jon chooses to privilege personal agency over social structure in his view of the world, and an analysis of structural enablement or constraint, as the case may be, is not the main message he wants readers, people with disabilities especially, to take away from his story. Rather he wants readers to know that all his life he has been on the lookout for people who could help him, and to his delight and benefit he has always found them. Therefore, when Jon encourages young people with disabilities to demand the very best of themselves, he advises them to seek out those "who believe in you and get the support you need," including other "people with disabilities who can help show you by example how to accomplish the things that you think are impossible." In this regard, we think that Stella may have said it best when she told us of the time that Jon told her son Cody that he had the ability to go to college: One sentence," she said, "changed his life" (chapter 5).

MULTICULTURALISM AND THE AMERICAN DREAM

In the course of our conversations with Jon and the writing of this book, the idea of the American dream emerged as a concept that was important to his understanding of self, which he defined in terms of his quest to achieve what he calls the tripod of success, a synergistic integration of "home life, education, and occupation." It also was a notion that seemed to be conflated with his feeling of patriotism for the United States, and we realized it was something we needed to further explore. At one point Ron asked Jon to reflect upon his patriotism in light of his disclosure that he may have acquired his cerebral palsy from his father's exposure to Agent Orange during the Vietnam War. To begin with, Jon said he will never know for sure if this is the case: "Like with almost anything in life, uncertainty will remain." But he made a distinction between patriotism and Americana. "Patriotism is more of a belief in the government, whereas Americana is the belief in the people and ideals of the country. In the last analysis, I don't care how my CP came to be. I just don't. Americana means something different to me."

For Jon, to speak of Americana or the American dream essentially amounts to the same thing. But the latter affords us another opportunity to situate Jon's life in broader context. To begin with, recall that the notion of the American dream is attributed to the social historian James Truslow Adams (1931), who described a vision of the United States as a society that was open to individual achievement. We have already noted the need to expand this vision beyond the narrow dream of financial success, but there are more important implications to pursue, which include a need to return to the concept of ableism.

In its simplest form, as we noted earlier, ableism entails a preference for able-bodiedness, but in its most radical form "defines the baseline of humanness" and assumes that quality of life cannot be achieved with a disabled body (Siebers 2008:8; see chapter 1). It is the complaint about this assumption that becomes the basis of the disability studies critique of the medical model, which aims to administer rehabilitative treatments to people with disabilities (when available), but which nonetheless assumes that disability is an inferior state of being. Research shows, for example, that the large majority of medical professionals believe that people with quadriplegia can expect to have a poor quality of life; in some cases, as if to say, a life that is not worth living (Gerhart et al. 1994; Gill 2000; Longmore 2003). On the other hand, the same research finds that the large majority of people with quadri-plegia say they have an average or above-average quality of life. Other stud-ies, too, find that medical professionals significantly underestimate the qual-ity of life of people with disabilities compared to the assessments of disabled people themselves. Of particular concern is that "these inaccurate and pessi-mistic professional views . . . are implicitly conveyed to patients and their families" while they are in the midst of making difficult decisions about how to respond to a congenital or newly acquired disability (Gill 2000). Hence the complaint about the story line of *Million Dollar Baby*, which suggested that euthanasia may be the most humane response to quadriplegia (chapter 1).

In the final analysis, people with disabilities do not wish to be constantly walking around with the unasked question, as W.E.B. Du Bois (1903) fa-mously observed of black people in America, "How does it feel to be a problem?" As Tobin Siebers (2008) reminds us, it is almost always true that people with disabilities have a better chance of enjoying a fulfilling life if they accept their disability as a positive identity and sometimes contentious way of being embodied in the world.

It is this idea that brings us to what Baker (2011) calls the *celebration* agenda of the disability rights movement, that is, the appreciation of disabil-ity as a valued form of social difference, akin to appreciating other forms of diversity such as those based on race, ethnicity, and sexual orientation. This is one of the key elements of the *cultural* model of disability, which views disability as a site of resistance to socially constructed notions of normality. [1] As Simi Linton observes:

> The cultural narrative of this community incorporates a fair share of adversity and struggle, but it is also, and significantly, an account of the world negotiat-ed from the vantage point of the atypical. Although the dominant culture describes that atypical experience as deficit and loss, the disabled commu-nity's narrative is the creative response to atypical experience, the adaptive maneuvers through a world configured for nondisabled people. The material that binds us is the art of finding one another, identifying and naming disability in a world reluctant to discuss it, and of unearthing historically and culturally significant material that relates to our experience. (1998:5)

In this way, the celebration agenda asserts its affinity with a broader vision of *multiculturalism*, a movement of respect and appreciation of human differ-ence as the essential feature of humanity (Alexander 2006; Berger 2012a; Gilson and DePoy 2000).

Multiculturalism, as a form of social inclusion in human societies, may be contrasted with other forms of inclusion that designate the criteria of social solidarity that defines *who belongs* and *who does not belong* to the group. According to Jeffrey Alexander, the core foundation of all "societies mani-fest distinctive racial, linguistic, religious, and geographical origins," and they establish their own "primordial qualities . . . as the highest criteria of humanity, as representing a higher competence for civil life. Only people of a certain race, who speak a certain language, who practice a certain religion, who make love in a certain manner, and who have immigrated from a certain part of the globe"—and we would add, possess a certain physical or cognitive ability—"only these very special persons actually possess what it takes to be members of our ideal society" (2006:405). At the same time, in democratic societies infused with the liberal values of the Enlightenment, "members of core groups can be—and often have been—convinced that beneath these differences, and even because of them, there exists a common humanity worthy of civil respect," and under certain circumstances social minorities, disabled people included, can be incorporated into the core or mainstream society (p. 405).

In the *assimilation* mode of incorporation, for example, inclusion is permitted as long as marginalized persons are able to shed their "polluted" qualities and act like the "rest of us." With some degree of rehabilitative treatment and social accommodation, therefore, disabled people can be enabled to act like nondisabled people and assimilated into mainstream society. But under an ableist regime of assimilation, the criteria that constitute normality vs. abnormality remain unchallenged. In other words, disabled *people* may be assimilate but disabled *qualities* may not.

In multiculturalism, on the other hand, which Alexander understands as a "moral preference," the conventional criteria for inclusion are disrupted, expanded, and transformed; that is, the qualities that were once relegated to the margins are used to reconfigure the core (2006:451). This is the essence of the social model of disability, which postulates that it is not an individual's impairment but the socially imposed barriers—the inaccessible buildings, the limited modes of communication and transportation, the prejudicial attitudes—that construct disability as a subordinate social status and devalued life experience.

In this regard, the concept of "universal design," which emerged in the 1970s, has been one way of thinking about how to construct a built environment that is accessible to and inclusive of people with disabilities. A concept whose origin is credited to architect Ronald Mace, who was a victim of polio (Woodward 2008), universal design is traditionally associated with the field of architecture, but it has been expanded to encompass questions of access to information and communication technologies as well as curricula and pedagogical practices in schools (Argondizza 2007; Burgstahler and Cory 2008; Jaeger 2012).

In the field of education, for instance, more and more teachers are coming to appreciate the importance of applying principles of universal design to develop alternative pedagogies to make learning more accessible to people of different learning styles. Similarly, in the workplace, we are coming to understand that an accessible workplace entails more than just physical accessibility. As one mobility-impaired professional told Dana Wilson-Kovacs and colleagues, speaking of the lowered expectations her employers have of her and other disabled employees that limit their opportunities for career advancement: "Just because you can get your wheelchair in the building doesn't necessarily mean you can still participate" (2008:712).

In a study of blind and vision-impaired employees, too, Mala Naraine and Peter Lindsay (2011) found that even when employers make workplace accommodations, visually impaired employees often have difficulty networking with other workers, socializing after work, and attending work-related social events that would enable them to become integrated into the workplace culture. As we have seen, even in the social sciences, where academics pride themselves in thinking they understand the socially constructed nature of reality, the spatial-temporal organization of the professional conference, both in its formal and informal dimensions, is constituted by ableist assumptions and structures that remain an obstacle to full participation for people with disabilities like Jon (chapter 6).

Thus disability scholars have challenged universal designers to broaden their vision of what constitutes "livable" space, that is, a place that is welcoming of and "makes room" for everyone in society, where no one is expected to leave their disability "at the door," even if they can get into the building, and where everyone has the opportunity to achieve full civic competence (Gerber 2003). As an example, in federal court cases and Department of Justice settlements, the Americans with Disabilities Act of 1990 has been interpreted as requiring movie theaters not only to make their stadium-style seats accessible to wheelchair users, but also to ensure that the "line of sight" offers an unobstructed view—rather than being far off to the side or in the distant rear—that is comparable to what is available for nondisabled patrons. In essence, the ADA not only entitles wheelchair users to minimal physical access to these facilities, but also to an overall movie experience of inclusiveness (U.S. Department of Justice 2006).

We also need to think critically about the technology industry's efforts to redesign products in ways that offer little new use value but only satisfy the interests of corporate profit-makers or the symbolic needs of consumption-hungry consumers. While technology has been a blessing for people with disabilities, the emphasis on constant innovation for the sake of innovation, rather than on universal design, often makes adaptable technology unnecessarily obsolete (Jaeger 2012; Morozov 2012). Even an updating of some minor software program may negatively affect the functioning of accessibility features that disabled people rely upon. In our conversations with parents at the AVA camp, parents expressed frustration that new designs for AAC equipment sometimes had less functional utility for their children than old designs. Writing about technology, Robert Merton was undoubtedly correct when he observed that "ours is a civilization committed to the quest for continually improved means to carelessly examined ends" (1967:vi; see also Ellul 1967).

More generally, with regards to users of AAC, full social inclusion in a multicultural society will require greater awareness and sensitivity to the intricacies of interpersonal communication. As we discovered through our experiences with Jon, there were a number of instances when we were uncertain as to how to proceed, such as what was the appropriate protocol for speaking with Jon in a group context, that is, should others stop talking at the point Jon wanted to enter the conversation but before he had completed his audio input, or should they continue talking until he was ready to speak? There is no simple answer to this question, but acknowledging the uncertainty seems a necessary precondition for satisfactory interactive outcomes.

In a study of wheelchair users' interactions with nondisabled others in public places, Spencer Cahill and Robin Eggleston (1995) shed light on this issue. They found that awkward encounters between nondisabled and disabled people often stem not from malicious intent but from uncertainty of what is expected. For example, should a nondisabled person offer assistance to someone who uses a wheelchair by opening a door for them or asking them if they need help retrieving something from a shelf in a grocery store? Cahill and Eggleston found that able-bodied people sometimes feared being rebuked for thinking that a wheelchair user might need help, finding "that they have judged [them] less competent than [they] wanted to be considered or consider themselves" (p. 693).

The question of uncertainty in interactions between disabled and nondisabled people is also raised by Michael Lenney and Howard Sercombe in their research on the phenomenon of staring, which we introduced earlier when we noted that nondisabled people often feel a "conflict between the 'desire to stare' and the 'desire not to stare'" at disability differences (2002:8; see chapter 6). On the one hand, it is impolite to stare; on the other hand, it is impolite to act as if the disabled person is invisible.[2] As Lenney and Sercombe observe:

> Choosing to interact or not to interact requires a complex level of communication, both visually and verbally. This complexity requires mindful maneuvering. In some cases, when interacting or not, people choose to mask their intentions and motivations for their behavior. Therefore, at an individual level, it is recommended that people attempt to observe what motivates them to avoid or associate with people who are different. At a social level, it is recommended people carefully attempt to interact with people who are assumed to be different, with the aim of diffusing constructed stereotypes. (p. 17)

People with disabilities do not want to be stereotyped and objectified, especially in terms of a negative social type, but neither do they want to be ignored. Jon Feucht will not be ignored. As he has said, "I am someone who demands to be noticed. I don't try to blend into the background and pretend that I, and my differences, don't exist. I want to be someone whom others take into account."

But if we are to understand Jon's life in social context, this will only be possible for him and others who wish to follow in his footsteps, if what we learn from his experience at the margins of society can be used to transform the core. In the case not only of communication differences but also of other disability differences, this will require us to slow down, to find ways to resist our profit-oriented, efficiency-based culture, a task that demands nothing short of a cultural revolution. To this end, we aim to connect the disability rights movement to what Carl Honoré (2005) calls the "slow movement," which constitutes a profound challenge to some of the dilemmas of contemporary life. We live in an age where we worship at the altar of speed. We eat fast food rather than "slow cook" our meals. We no longer write letters or speak on the phone, but rather we text and tweet. We now try to spend "quality" time with our children to compensate for the diminishing "quantity" of time we have for them. We worry about the economy "finding time" for us, but at the expense of "finding time" for our families or ourselves. Is this what has become of the American dream?

It is in mounting a challenge to this state of affairs that disability studies and the disability rights movement is relevant to disabled and nondisabled people alike. By acquiring an empathic understanding of the disability experience, and learning to see the world through the eyes of people like Jon, we hope to advance a public conversation about rethinking and reconfiguring the strictures of ableist society in order to create a truly multicultural world. This project ultimately takes us to the heart of our vision of democracy, which Alexander argues should best be "understood as a participatory political community whose citizens display commitments to a public interest that transcends private and egoistic concerns . . . [and] can be sustained only if a sense of altruistic civic virtue" is able to permeate our cultural, political, and economic life (2006:45).

Clearly, we have a long way to go to realize this ideal. In a contemporary climate of culture conflict and mean-spiritedness, a political era of budget cuts and roll-backs in government services, and an economy marked by exacerbating inequality in the distribution of valued goods and services, it is arguably utopian to think that anything can be done to substantially reverse this state of affairs. Nevertheless, as Norman Denzin and Michael Giardina suggest (2012), this is the task that social science should commit itself to addressing. To do otherwise is to be complicit in the loss of opportunities to contribute to a better world. As for the particular circumstances of people with disabilities, we agree with Gary Albrecht and Michael Bury, who believe that the societal treatment of this constituency is a barometer by which the "moral health of a society" can be measured (2001:600). In this way, as Dan Goodley observes, disability studies is dedicated to the task of resisting "various signifiers of disabling society and the making of new signifiers for the understanding of self, culture and society," seeking not an erasure but an accommodation and appreciation of social difference (2011:170). Along with Carol Gill (1994), therefore, we hope for the day not when disability differences will be deemed irrelevant, but when they will provoke a respectful curiosity about what people with disabilities have learned that could make us all better citizens of the world.

NOTES

1. The cultural model also entails a critique of cultural representations that *dis*-locate people with disabilities (Goodley 2011; Snyder and Mitchell 2006).

2. Similarly, Hilde Zitzelsberger (2005) found that women with physical disabilities often felt they were only *visible* to others in terms of their impairment, but *invisible* in terms of their other attributes. One woman explained that she felt visible as a woman who "walked down the street with crutches," but invisible "as a woman that could have a relationship, as a woman that could be seen in a workplace, as a woman that could be a mother" (p. 45).

References

AAC Mentor Project. 2010. "What Is AAC?" AAC Mentor Project at Penn State, available at http://www.mcn.ed.psu.edu.

Adams, James Truslow. 1931. *The Epic of America*. Boston: Little, Brown.

Akamanti, Jeanie. 2004. "Back of the Bus? I Just Want on the Bus!" *SWS Network News* 21: 13–16.

Albrecht, Gary L., and Michael Bury. 2001. "The Political Economy of the Disability Marketplace." In *Handbook of Disability Studies*, eds. Gary L. Albrecht, Katherine D. Seelman, and Michael Bury. Thousand Oaks, CA: Sage.

Alexander, Jeffrey C. 1982. *Theoretical Logic in Sociology: Positivism, Presuppositions, and Current Controversies*. Berkeley: University of California Press.

———. 1988. *Action and Its Environments: Toward a New Synthesis*. New York: Columbia University Press.

———. 2006. *The Civil Sphere*. New York: Oxford University Press.

Argondizza, Thomas. 2007. "Tools for Universal Instruction." In *Building Pedagogical Curb Cuts: Incorporating Disability in the University Classroom and Curriculum*, eds. Liat Ben-Moshe, Rebecca C. Cory, Mia Feldbaum, and Ken Sagendorf. Syracuse, NY: Syracuse University Press.

Atkinson, Paul. 2013. "Ethnographic Writing, the Avant-Garde and a Failure of Nerve." *International Review of Qualitative Research* 6: 19–36.

Atkinson, Robert. 1998. *The Life Story Interview*. Thousand Oaks, CA: Sage.

Baker, Bernadette. 2002. "The Hunt for Disability: The New Eugenics and the Normalization of School-Children." *Teachers College Record* 104: 663–703.

Baker, Bruce. 2005. "Let's Not Go Back to the Flintstones." *Speak Up*, 20 (2): 13, available at http://www.ussaac.org.

Baker, Dana Lee. 2011. *The Politics of Neurodiversity: Why Public Policy Matters*. Boulder, CO: Lynne Rienner.

Bandura, Albert. 1997. *Self-Efficacy: The Exercise of Control*. New York: W. H. Freeman.

Barnes, Colin, and Geof Mercer. 2001. "Disability Culture: Assimilation or Inclusion?" In *Handbook of Disability Studies*, eds. Gary L. Albrecht, Katherine D. Seelman, and Michael Bury. Thousand Oaks, CA: Sage.

Barnes, Colin, and Alison Sheldon. 2010. "Disability, Politics and Poverty in a Majority World Context." *Disability & Society* 25: 771–782.

Barth, John. 1968. *Lost in the Funhouse: Fiction for Print, Tape, Live Voice*. New York: Doubleday.

Barton, Len, and Felicity Armstrong. 2001. "Disability, Education, and Inclusion: Cross-Cultural Issues and Dilemmas." In *Handbook of Disability Studies*, eds. Gary L. Albrecht, Katherine D. Seelman, and Michael Bury. Thousand Oaks, CA: Sage.

Bedrosian, J. L., L. A. Hoag, D. Johnson, and S. N. Calculator. 1998. "Communicative Competence as Perceived by Adults with Severe Speech Impairments Associated with Cerebral Palsy." *Journal of Speech, Language and Hearing Research* 41: 667–675.

Bergen, Marja. 1999. *Riding the Roller Coaster: Living with Mood Disorders*. Kelowna, British Columbia: Wood Lake.

Berger, Ronald J. 2008a. "Agency, Structure, and the Transition to Disability: A Case Study with Implications for Life History Research." *The Sociological Quarterly* 49: 303–333.

———. 2008b. "Disability and the Dedicated Wheelchair Athlete: Beyond the 'Supercrip' Critique." *Journal of Contemporary Ethnography* 37: 647–678.

———. 2009. *Hoop Dreams on Wheels: Disability and the Competitive Wheelchair Athlete*. New York: Routledge.

———. 2012a. *The Holocaust, Religion, and the Politics of Collective Memory: Beyond Sociology*. New Brunswick, NJ: Transaction.

———. 2012b. "What's So Funny about Disability?" *The Society Pages* (Dec. 26), available at http://thesocietypages.org.

———. 2013. *Introducing Disability Studies*. Boulder, CO: Lynne Rienner.

Berger, Ronald J., Carla Corroto, Jennifer Flad, and Richard Quinney. 2013. "Navigating the Terrain of Medical Diagnosis and Treatment: Patient Decision Making and Uncertainty." In *Studies in Symbolic Interaction*, vol. 40, ed. Norman K. Denzin. Bingley, UK: Emerald.

Berger, Ronald J., and Jon Feucht. 2012. "'Thank You for Your Words': Observations from a Disability Summer Camp." *Qualitative Inquiry* 18: 76–85.

———. 2013. "Travels with Jon and Sarah: A Journey to and Through the Eighth International Congress of Qualitative Inquiry." *International Review of Qualitative Research* 6: 57–78.

Berger, Ronald J., and Richard Quinney (eds.). 2005. *Storytelling Sociology: Narrative as Social Inquiry*. Boulder, CO: Lynne Rienner.

Berger, Ronald J., David Travis, and Jon Feucht. 2012. "Overcoming Discomfort with Disability." *The Society Pages* (Sept. 28), available at http://thesocietypages.org.

Beukelman, David R., and Pat Mirenda. 2012. *Augmentative and Alternative Communication: Supporting Children and Adults with Complex Communication Needs*. 3rd ed. Baltimore, MD: Paul H. Brookes.

Bliss, Charles. 1978. *Semantography: Blissymbolics*. 3rd ed. Sydney: Semantography-Blissymbolics Publications.

Blissymbolics Communication International. n.d. "Welcome to BCI," http://www.blissymbolics.org.

Bochner, Arthur P. 2001. "Narrative's Virtues." *Qualitative Inquiry* 7: 131–157.

Bogdan, Robert. 1988. *Freak Show: Presenting Human Oddities for Amusement and Profit*. Chicago: University of Chicago Press.

Braddock, David L., and Susan L. Parish. 2001. "An Institutional History of Disability." In *Handbook of Disability Studies*, eds. Gary L. Albrecht, Katherine D. Seelman, and Michael Bury. Thousand Oaks, CA: Sage.

Branfield, Fran. 1998. "What Are You Doing Here? 'Non-disabled' People and the Disability Movement." *Disability & Society* 13: 143–144.

Brownlee, Alia. n.d. "Augmentative Communication: An Overview of ALS and Assistive Technology." ALS Association, available at http://www.alsa.org.

Bruner, Jerome. 2004. "Life as Narrative." *Social Research* 7: 691–710.

Burgstahler, Sheryl A., and Rebecca C. Cory (eds.). 2008. *Universal Design in Higher Education: From Principles to Practice*. Cambridge, MA: Harvard Education Press.

Bury, Michael. 2000. "On Chronic Illness and Disability." In *Handbook of Disability Studies*, eds. Gary L. Albrecht, Katherine D. Seelman, and Michael Bury. Thousand Oaks, CA: Sage.

Cahill, Spencer E., and Robin Eggleston. 1994. "Managing Emotions in Public: The Case of Wheelchair Users." *Social Psychology Quarterly* 57: 300–312.

———. 1995. "Reconsidering the Stigma of Physical Disability: Wheelchair Use and Public Kindness." *The Sociological Quarterly* 36: 681–698.

Carr, David. 1986. *Time, Narrative, and History*. Bloomington: Indiana University Press.

Cassell, Catherine, and Phil Johnson. 2006. "Action Research: Explaining the Diversity." *Human Relations* 59: 783–814.

Caton, Sue, and Carolyn Kagan. 2007. "Comparing Transition Expectations of Young People with Moderate Learning Disabilities with Other Vulnerable Youth and with Their Non-disabled Counterparts." *Disability & Society* 22: 473–488.

Cerebral Palsy Source. 2013. "Athetoid Cerebral Palsy," available at http://www.cerebralpalsysource.com.

Charlton, James I. 1998. *Nothing About Us Without Us: Disability Oppression and Empowerment*. Berkeley: University of California Press.

Charmaz, Kathy. 2012. "Mixing or Adding Methods? An Exploration and Critique." In *Qualitative Inquiry and the Politics of Advocacy*, eds. Norman K. Denzin and Michael D. Giardina. Walnut Creek, CA: Left Coast Press.

Clandinin, D. Jean. 2013. *Engaging in Narrative Inquiry*. Walnut Creek, CA: Left Coast Press.

Clarke, K., H. McConachie, K. Price, and P. Wood. 2001. "Views of Young People Using Augmentative and Alternative Communication Systems." *International Journal of Language and Communication Disorders* 36: 107–115.

Connor, David J., and Beth A. Ferri. 2007. "The Conflict Within: Resistance to Inclusion and Other Paradoxes in Special Education." *Disability & Society* 22: 63–77.

Cornell University. 2013. "Disability Statistics: Online Resources of U.S. Disability Statistics," available at http://www.disabilitystatistics.org.

Couser, G. Thomas. [2005] 2013. "Disability, Life Narrative, and Representation." In *The Disability Studies Reader*, 4th ed., ed. Lennard Davis. New York: Routledge.

Creech, Richard D. 1992. *Reflections from a Unicorn*. Bilpin, New South Wales: R C Publishing.

Danforth, Scot. 2009. *The Incomplete Child: An Intellectual History of Learning Disabilities*. New York: Peter Lang.

Darling, Rosalyn Benjamin. 2000. "Only for Individuals with Disabilities?" ASA *Footnotes* (May/June): 6.

Davis, Lennard J. 2001. "Identity Politics, Disability, and Culture." In *Handbook of Disability Studies*, eds. Gary L. Albrecht, Katherine D. Seelman, and Michael Bury. Thousand Oaks, CA: Sage.

———. 2005. "Why Disability Studies Matters*." Inside Higher Ed* (Feb. 21), available at http://www.insidehighered.com.

Deal, Mark. 2003. "Disabled People's Attitudes toward Other Impairment Groups: A Hierarchy of Impairments." *Disability & Society* 18: 897–910.

DeJong, Gerben, and Ian Basnett. 2001. "Disability and Health Policy: The Role of Markets in the Delivery of Health Services." In *Handbook of Disability Studies*. eds. Gary L. Albrecht, Katherine D. Seelman, and Michael Bury. Thousand Oaks, CA: Sage.

Delamont, Sara. 2013. "Performing Research or Researching Performance?" *International Review of Qualitative Research* 6: 1–18.

Denzin, Norman K. 1989. *Interpretive Biography*. Newbury Park, CA: Sage.

———. 1998. "The New Ethnography." *Journal of Contemporary Ethnography* 27: 405–415.

Denzin, Norman K., and Michael D. Giardina (eds.). 2012. *Qualitative Inquiry and the Politics of Advocacy*. Walnut Creek, CA: Left Coast Press.

Du Bois, W. E. B. [1903] 1996. *The Souls of Black Folk*. New York: Penguin.

Duckett, Paul. S. 1998. "What Are You Doing Here? 'Non-disabled' People and the Disability Movement: A Response to Fran Branfield." *Disability & Society* 13: 625–628.

Eisenstadt, Stuart N. 1956. *From Generation to Generation: Age Groups and Social Structures*. New York: Free Press.

Elder, Glen. 1995. "The Life Course Paradigm: Social Change and Individual Development." In *Examining Lives in Context: Perspectives on the Ecology of Human Development*, eds. Jeylan T. Mortimer and Michael J. Shanahan. New York: Springer.

Ellensen, Richard. 2005. "In the Camp of Depression" (interview with Jon Feucht). *SpeakUP* 20 (2): 5, 7, 18.

Ellis, Carolyn, and Jerry Rawicki. 2013. "Collaborative Witnessing of Survival During the Holocaust: An Exemplar of Relational Autoethnography." *Qualitative Inquiry* 19: 366– 380.

Ellul, Jacques. [1964] 1967. *The Technological Society*. New York: Vintage.

Engel, David M., and Frank W. Munger. 2003. *Rights of Inclusion: Law and Identity in the Life Stories of Americans with Disabilities*. Chicago: University of Chicago Press.

Erickson, J. David, 1997. "Testimony on Birth Defects Among Vietnam Veterans' Children." House Veteran's Affairs, Subcommittee on Hospitals and Health Care (Apr. 16), available at http://www.hhs.gov.

Feucht, Jon. 2003a. "American Values in AAC: One Man's Vision." 2003 Edwin and Esther Prentke AAC Distinguished Lecturer Speech, available at http://www.aacinstitute.org.

———. 2003b. *The Tan Car*. Madison, WI: Omni Press.

———. 2004. *Straight Talks: Talks on Disability Issues*. Madison, WI: Omni Press.

———. 2006. *Keys to Special Education Success: A Student's View*. Unpublished master's thesis, Department of Special Education, University of Wisconsin-Whitewater.

Fine, Michelle, and Adrienne Asch. 1988. "Disability Beyond Stigma: Social Interaction, Discrimination, and Activism." *Journal of Social Issues* 44: 3–21.

Flad, Jennifer, Ronald J. Berger, and Jon Feucht. 2011. "Can You Hear Me Now? Augmentative Communication, Methodological Empowerment, and the Life Story of Jon Feucht." *Disability Studies Quarterly* 31 (4), available at http://dsq-sds.org.

Fleischer, Doris Zames, and Frieda Zames. 2001. *The Disability Rights Movement: From Charity to Confrontation*. Philadelphia: Temple University Press.

Frank, Arthur. 1995. *The Wounded Storyteller: Body, Illness, and Ethics*. Chicago: University of Chicago Press.

Fries, Kenny (ed.). 1997. *Staring Back: The Disability Experience from the Inside Out*. New York: Plume.

Galvin, Ruth. 2003. "The Paradox of Disability Culture: The Need to Combine versus the Imperative to Let Go." *Disability & Society* 18: 675–690.

Gecas, Viktor. 1989. "The Social Psychology of Self-Efficacy." *Annual Review of Sociology* 15: 291–316.

Geralis, Elaine. 1991. *Children with Cerebral Palsy: A Parent's Guide*. Bethesda, MD: Woodbine House.

Gerber, Elaine. 2003. "Livable Communities Throughout the Life Course." *Disability Studies Quarterly* 23: 41–57.

Gerhart, Kenneth A., Jane Kozoil-McLain, Steven R. Lowenstein, and Gale G. Whiteneck. 1994. "Quality of Life Following Spinal Cord Injury: Knowledge and Attitudes of Emergency Care Providers." *Annals of Emergency Medicine* 23: 807–812.

Giddens, Anthony. 1984. *The Constitution of Society: Outline of the Theory of Structuration*. Berkeley: University of California Press.

Gill, Carol J. 1994. "Questioning Continuum." In *The Ragged Edge: The Disability Experience from the Pages of the First Fifteen Years of the Disability Rag*, ed. Barrett Shaw. Louisville, KY: Advocado Press.

———. 2000. "Health Professionals, Disability, and Assisted Suicide: An Examination of Relevant Empirical Evidence and Reply to Batavia." *Psychology, Public Policy, and Law* 6: 526–545.

———. 2001. "Divided Understandings: The Social Experience of Disability." In *Handbook of Disability Studies*, eds. Gary L. Albrecht, Katherine D. Seelman, and Michael Bury. Thousand Oaks, CA: Sage.

Gilson, Stephen French, and Elizabeth DePoy. 2000. "Multiculturalism and Disability: A Critical Perspective." *Disability & Society* 15: 207–217.

Glaser, Barney G., and Anselm L. Strauss. 1967. *The Discovery of Grounded Therory*. Chicago: Aldine.

Glenn, Evelyn N. 2010. *Forced to Care: Coercion and Caregiving*. Cambridge, MA: Harvard University Press.

Glennen, Sharon L. 1997. "Introduction to Augmentative and Alternative Communication Systems." In *Handbook of Augmentative and Alternative Communication*, eds. Sharon Glennen and Denise C. DeCoste. San Diego, CA: Singular Publishing Group.

Goetting, Ann. 1995. "Fictions of the Self." In *Individual Voices, Collective Visions: Fifty Years of Women in Sociology*, eds. Ann Goetting and Sarah Fenstermaker. Philadelphia: Temple University Press.

Goffman, Erving. 1963. *Stigma: Notes on the Management of Spoiled Identity*. Englewood Cliffs, NJ: Prentice-Hall.

Goodley, Dan. 2011. *Disability Studies: An Interdisciplinary Introduction*. London: Sage.

Grossman, Francis Kaplan. 1972. *Brothers and Sisters of Retarded Children*. New York: Syracuse University Press.

Gusdorf, Georges. 1980. "Conditions and Limits of Autobiography." In *Autobiography: Essays Theoretical and Critical*, ed. J. Olney. Princeton, NJ: Princeton University Press.

Haller, Beth A. 2010. *Representing Disability in an Ableist World*. Louisville, KY: Advocado Press.

Harris, Jennifer. 2010. "The Use, Role and Application of Advanced Technology in the Lives of Disabled People in the UK." *Disability & Society* 25: 427–439.

Higginbotham, D. J., H. Shane, S. Russell, and K. Caves. 2007. "Access to AAC: Present, Past, and Future." *Augmentative and Alternative Communication* 23: 243–257.

Hill, Katya, and Barry Romich. 2002. "A Rate Index for Augmentative and Alternative Communication." *International Journal of Speech Technology* 5: 57–64.

Hoag, Linda, Jan L. Bedrosian, Kathleen F. McCoy, and Dallas E. Johnson. 2004. "Trade-Offs Between Informativeness and Speed of Message Delivery in Augmentative and Alternative Communication." *Journal of Speech, Language, and Hearing Research* 47: 1270–1285.

Hodge, Suzanne. 2007. "Why Is the Potential of Augmentative and Alternative Communication Not Being Realized? Exploring the Experiences of People Who Use Communication Aids." *Disability & Society* 22: 457–471.

Hogan, Dennis. 2012. *Family Consequences of Children's Disabilities*. New York: Russell Sage Foundation.

Holland, Daniel. 2006. "Franklin D. Roosevelt's Shangri-La: Foreshadowing the Independent Living Movement in Warm Springs, Georgia, 1926–1945." *Disability & Society* 21: 513–535.

Honoré, Carl. 2005. *In Praise of Slowness: How a Worldwide Movement Is Challenging the Cult of Speed*. London: Orion.

Hou, Mei, Jian-Hui Zhao, and Rong Yu. 2006. "Recent Advances in Dyskenetic Cerebral Palsy." *World Journal of Pediatrics* 2: 23–28.

Hughes, Bill, and Kevin Paterson. 1997. "The Social Model of Disability and the Disappearing Body: Towards a Sociology of Impairment." *Disability & Society* 12: 325–340.

Jacobs, B., R. Drew, B. T. Ogletree, and K. Pierce. 2004. "Augmentative and Alternative Communication (AAC) for Adults with Severe Aphasia: Where We Stand and How We Can Go Further." *Disability and Rehabilitation* 26: 1231–1240.

Jaeger, Paul. 2012. *Disability and the Internet: Confronting a Digital Divide*. Boulder, CO: Lynne Rienner.

Jamison, Kay Redfield. 1995. *An Unquiet Mind: A Memoir of Moods and Madness*. New York: Alfred Knopf.

Jans, D., and S. Clark. 1998. "High Technology Aids to Communication." In *Augmentative Communication in Practice: An Introduction*, ed. Allan Wilson. Edinburgh: University of Edinburgh.

Jones, Martha Wilson, Elaine Morgan, and Jean E. Shelton. 2007. "Cerebral Palsy: Introduction and Diagnosis." *Journal of Pediatric Health Care* 21: 146–152.

Joseph, Frederick K., and Kay Redfield Jamison. 2007. *Manic-Depressive Illness: Bipolar Disorders*. Oxford: Oxford University Press.

Juette, Melvin, and Ronald J. Berger. 2008. *Wheelchair Warrior: Gangs, Disability, and Basketball*. Philadelphia: Temple University Press.

Killacky, John R. 2004. "Careening toward Kensho: Ruminations on Disability and Community." In *Queer Crips: Disabled Gay Men and Their Stories*, eds. Bob Guter and John R. Killacky. New York: Haworth Press.

King, Jesse. 2012. "Birth Defects Caused by Agent Orange." *Embryo Project Encyclopedia*, Arizona State University, available at http://embryo.asu.edu.

Kitchin, Rob. 2000. "The Researched Opinions on Research: Disabled People and Disability Research." *Disability & Society* 15: 25–47.

Kittay, Eva Feder, and Ellen K. Kittay (eds.). 2002. *The Subject of Care: Feminist Perspectives on Dependency*. Lanham, MD: Rowman & Littlefield.

Krumer-Nevo, Michal. 2012. "Writing against Othering." In *Qualitative Inquiry and the Politics of Advocacy*, eds. Norman K. Denzin and Michael D. Giardina. Walnut Creek, CA: Left Coast Press.

Landsman, Gail Heidi. 2009. *Reconstructing Motherhood and Disability in the Age of "Perfect" Babies.* New York: Routledge.

Lasker, J. P., & Bedrosian, J. L. 2001. "Promoting Acceptance of Augmentative and Alternative Communication by Adults with Acquired Communication Disorders." *Augmentative and Alternative Communication* 17: 141–153.

Leiter, Valerie. 2007. "'Nobody's Just Normal, You Know': The Social Creation of Developmental Disability." *Social Science & Medicine* 65: 1630–1641.

———. 2012. *Their Time Has Come: Youth with Disabilities Entering Adulthood*. New Brunswick, NJ: Rutgers University Press.

Lenney, Michael, and Howard Sercombe. 2002. "'Did You See That Guy in the Wheelchair Down in the Pub?' Interactions across Difference in a Public Place." *Disability & Society* 17: 5–18.

Linton, Simi. 1998. *Claiming Disability: Knowledge and Identity*. New York: New York University Press.

Lipsky, Dorothy Kezner, and Alan Gartner. 1997. *Inclusion and School Reform: Transforming America's Classroom*. Baltimore: Paul H. Brookes.

Longmore, Paul K. 2003. *Why I Burned My Books and Other Essays on Disability*. Philadelphia: Temple University Press.

Luken, Paul. C., and Suzanne Vaughan. 1999. "Life History and the Critique of American Sociological Practice." *Sociological Inquiry* 69: 404–425.

Marshak, Laura E., Milton Seligman, and Fran Prezant. 1999. *Disability and the Family Life Cycle*. New York: Basic Books.

Maslow, Abraham. 1954. *Motivation and Personality*. New York: Harper.

McRuer, Robert. 2006. *Crip Theory: Cultural Signs of Queerness and Disability*. New York: New York University Press.

———. [2002] 2010. "Compulsory Able-Bodiedness and Queer/Disabled Existence." In *The Disability Studies Reader*, 3rd ed., ed. Lennard Davis. New York: Routledge.

Mekdeci, Betty. 2007. "Agent Orange and Birth Defects." *The VVA Veteran* (Nov./Dec.), available at http://www.vva.org.

Merton, Robert K. 1938. "Social Structure and Anomie." *American Sociological Review* 3: 672– 682.

———. 1967. "Forward" to Jacques Ellul, *The Technological Society*. New York: Vintage.

Messner, Steven F., and Richard Rosenfeld. 2001. *Crime and the American Dream*. 3rd ed. Belmont, CA: Wadsworth.

Meyer, Donald J. (ed.). 1995. *Uncommon Fathers: Reflections on Raising a Child with a Disability*. Bethesda, MD: Woodbine House.

Meyer, Maonna Harrington (ed.). 2000. *Care Work: Gender, Class, and the Welfare State*. New York: Routledge.

Meyer, Michelle, Michelle Donelly, and Patricia Weerakoon. 2007. "'They're Taking the Place of My Hands': Perspectives of People Using Personal Care." *Disability & Society* 22: 595–608.

Millar, D. C., J. C. Light, and R. W. Schlosser. 2006. "The Impact of Augmentative and Alternative Communication Intervention on the Speech Production of Individuals with Developmental Disabilities: A Research Review." *Journal of Speech, Language and Hearing Research* 49: 248–264.

Miller, Freeman, and Steven J. Bachrach. 1995. *Cerebral Palsy: A Complete Guide for Caregiving*. Baltimore: Johns Hopkins University Press.

Miller, Nancy B., and Catherine C. Sammons. 1999. *Everybody's Different: Understanding and Changing Our Reactions to Disabilities*. Baltimore: Paul H. Brookes.

Mills, C. Wright. 1959. *The Sociological Imagination*. New York: Oxford University Press.

Morozov, Evgeny. 2012. "Form and Fortune: Steve Job's Pursuit of Perfection—and the Consequences." *The New Republic* (Mar. 15): 18–27.

Murphy, Robert. 1987. *The Body Silent*. New York: Henry Holt.

Naraine, Mala D., and Peter H. Lindsay. 2011. "Social Inclusion of Employees Who Are Blind or Low Vision." *Disability & Society* 26: 389–403.

Naseef, Robert A. 2001. *Special Children, Challenged Parents: The Struggles and Rewards of Raising a Child with a Disability*. Baltimore, MD: Paul H. Brookes.

National Institute of Mental Health. 2008. "Bipolar Disorder," available at http://www.nimh.hih.gov.

Neumann, Anna. 1997. "Ways without Words: Learning from Silence and Story in Post-Holocaust Lives." In *Learning from Our Lives: Women, Research, and Autobiography in Education*, eds. Anna Neumann and L. Penelope Peterson. New York: Teachers College Press.

Noddings, Nel. 1984. *Caring: A Feminine Approach to Ethics and Moral Education*. Berkeley: University of California Press.

Nowell, Nefertiti L. 2006. "Oppression." In *Encyclopedia of Disability*, vol. 3, ed. Gary L. Albrecht. Thousand Oaks, CA: Sage.

Oakley, Ann. 2010. "The Social Science of Biographical Life-writing: Some Methodological and Ethical Issues." *International Journal of Social Research Methodology* 13: 425–439.

Ochs, Elinor, and Lisa Capps. 2001. *Living Narrative: Creating Lives in Everyday Storytelling*. Cambridge, MA: Harvard University Press.

Oliver, Michael. 1990. *The Politics of Disablement*. New York: Macmillan.

———. 1992. "Changing the Social Relations of Research Production." *Disability, Handicap and Society* 7: 101–114.

———. 1997. "Emancipatory Research: Realistic Goal or Impossible Dream?" In *Doing Disability Research*, eds. Colin Barnes and George Mercer. Leeds, UK: Disability Press.

Papadimitriou, Christina. 2001. "From Dis-ability to Difference: Conceptual and Methodological Issues in the Study of Physical Disability." In *Handbook of Phenomenology and Medicine*, ed. S. Kay Toombs. Netherlands: Kluwer Academic.

———. 2008a. "The 'I' of the Beholder: Phenomenological Seeing in Disability Research." *Sport, Ethics, and Philosophy* 2: 216–233.

———. 2008b. "'It Was Hard But You Did It': The Co-Production of 'Work' in a Clinical Setting Among Spinal Cord Injured Adults and Their Physical Therapists." *Disability and Rehabilitation* 30: 365–374.

Papadimitriou, Christina, and David A. Stone. 2011. "Addressing Existential Disruption in Traumatic Spinal Cord Injury: A New Approach to Human Temporality in Inpatient Rehabilitation." *Disability and Rehabilitation* 33: 2121–2133.

Peters, Jeremy W. 2005. "In Wisconsin, Fallout Grows over Decision on Pageant." *New York Times* (Apr. 6), available at http://www.nytimes.com.

Petersen, Amy J. 2011. "Research with Individuals Labeled 'Other': Reflections on the Research Process." *Disability & Society* 26: 293–305.

Pincus, Fred. 2011. *Understanding Diversity: An Introduction to Class, Race, Gender, Sexual Orientation, and Disability*. Boulder, CO: Lynne Rienner.

Plummer, Ken. 2001. *Documents of Life II: An Invitation to a Critical Humanism*. Thousand Oaks, CA: Sage.

Polletta, Francesca, Pang Ching, Bobby Chen, Beth Gharrity Gardner, and Alice Motes. 2011. "The Sociology of Storytelling." *Annual Review of Sociology* 37: 109–130.

Potok, Andrew. 2002. *A Matter of Dignity: Changing the World of the Disabled*. New York: Bantam.

Rainey, Sarah Smith. 2011. *Love, Sex and Disability: The Pleasures of Care*. Boulder, CO: Lynne Rienner.

Ramazanoglu, Caroline, and Janet Holland. 2002. *Feminist Methodology: Challenges and Choices*. Thousand Oaks, CA: Sage.

Reinharz, Shulamit. 1992. *Feminist Methods in Social Research*. New York: Oxford University Press.

Rosenwald, George C., and Richard L. Ochberg (eds.). 1992. *Storied Lives: The Cultural Politics of Self-Understanding*. New Haven, CT: Yale University Press.

Rush, William. [1986] 2008. *Journey Out of Silence: An Autobiography*. Lulu.com.

Schlosser, Ralf W., Dorothy M. Blischak, and Rajinder K. Koul. 2003. "Roles of Speech Output in ACC." In *The Efficacy of Augmentative and Alternative Communication: Towards Evidence-Based Practice*, ed. Ralf W. Schlosser. San Diego, CA: Academic Press.

Schriner, Kay. 2001. "A Disability Studies Perspective on Employment Issues and Policies for Disabled People: An International View." In *Handbook of Disability Studies*, eds. Gary L. Albrecht, Katherine D. Seelman, and Michael Bury. Thousand Oaks, CA: Sage.

Scotch, Richard K., and Kay Schriner. 1997. "Disability as Human Variation: Implications for Policy." *The Annals of the American Academy of Political and Social Science* 549: 148–160.

Sewell, Jr., William H. 1992. "A Theory of Structure: Duality, Agency, and Transformation." *American Journal of Sociology* 98: 1–29.

Shakespeare, Tom. 2010. "The Social Model of Disability." In *The Disability Studies Reader*, 3rd ed., ed. Lennard Davis. New York: Routledge.

Shapiro, Joseph P. 1993. *No Pity: People with Disabilities Forging a New Civil Rights Movement*. New York: Times Books.

Sherry, Mark. 2004. "Overlaps and Contradictions Between Queer Theory and Disability Studies." *Disability & Society* 19: 769–783.

———. [2007] 2010. "(Post)colonizing Disability." In *The Disability Studies Reader*, 3rd ed., ed. Lennard Davis. New York: Routledge.

Siebers, Tobin. 2008. *Disability Theory*. Ann Arbor: University of Michigan Press.

Sigafoos, Jeff, and Eric Drasgow. 2001. "Conditional Use of Aided and Unaided AAC: A Clinical Review and Demonstration." *Focus on Autism and Other Developmental Disabilities* 16: 152–161.

Snyder, Sharon L., and David T. Mitchell. 2006. *Cultural Locations of Disability*. Chicago: University of Chicago Press.

Solomon, Andrew. 2012. *Far from the Tree; Parents, Children, and the Search for Identity*. New York: Scribner.

Stodden, R. A., and P. W. Dowrick. 2000. "Postsecondary Education and Employment of Adults with Disabilities." *American Rehabilitation* 25: 19–23.

Stoecker, Randy. 1999. "Are Academics Irrelevant? Roles for Scholars in Participatory Research." *American Behavioral Scientist* 42: 840–854.

Taylor, Daniel. 2001. *Tell Me a Story: The Life-Shaping Power of Stories*. St. Paul, MN: Bogg Walk.

Thomas, Carol. 2004. "How Is Disability Understood? An Examination of Sociological Approaches." *Disability & Society* 19: 569–583.

Thomas, W. I., and Florian Znaniecki. 1918–1920. *The Polish Peasant in Europe and America*. Vols. I and II., Chicago: University of Chicago Press.

Tillmann-Healy, Lisa M. 2003. "Friendship as Method." *Qualitative Inquiry* 9: 729–749.

Tollifson, Joan. 1997. "Imperfection Is a Beautiful Thing: On Disability and Meditation." In *Staring Back: The Disability Experience from the Inside Out*, ed. Kenny Fries. New York: Plume.

Turner, Bryan S. 2001. "Disability and the Sociology of the Body." In *Handbook of Disability Studies*, eds. Gary L. Albrecht, Katherine D. Seelman, and Michael Bury. Thousand Oaks, CA: Sage.

U.S. Department of Justice. 2006. "Federal Court Orders AMC Movie Theater Chain to Improve "Wheelchair Seating at AMC Theaters Nationwide" (Jan. 11), available at http://www.justice.gov.

Vanderheide, G. C. 2002. "A Journey through Early Augmentative Communication and Computer Access." *Journal of Rehabilitation Research and Development* 39: 39–53.

Watson, Nick. 2002. "Well, I Know This Is Going to Sound Very Strange to You, but I Don't See Myself as a Disabled Person: Identity and Disability." *Disability & Society* 17: 509–527.

Wedgwood, Nikki. 2011. "A Person with Abilities: The Transition to Adulthood of a Young Woman with a Severe Physical Impairment." *Young* 19: 433–452.

Wehmeyer, Michael L., and Sharon L. Field. 2007. *Self-Determination: Instructional and Assessment Strategies*. Thousand Oaks, CA: Corwin Press.

Weiss, Gail. 1999. *Body Images: Embodiment as Intercorporeality*. New York: Routledge.

White, Hayden. 1973. *Metahistory: The Historical Imagination in Nineteenth-Century Europe*. Baltimore: Johns Hopkins University Press.

Whittemore, Robert D., L. L. Langness, and Paul Koegel. 1986. "The Life History Approach to Mental Retardation." In *Culture and Retardation: Life Histories of Mildly Mentally Retarded Persons in American Society*, eds. L. L. Langness and Harold G. Levine. Dordrecht, Netherlands: D. Reidel.

Williams, Gareth. 2001. "Theorizing Disability." In *Handbook of Disability* Studies, eds. Gary L. Albrecht, Katherine D. Seelman, and Michael Bury. Thousand Oaks, CA: Sage.

Wilson-Kovacs, Dana, Michelle K. Ryan, S. Alexander Haslam, and Anna Rabinovich. 2008. "Just Because You Can Get a Wheelchair in the Building Doesn't Necessarily Mean That You Can Still Participate." *Disability & Society* 23: 705–717.

Winzer, Margret A., and Kaz Mazurek (eds.). 2000. *Special Education in the 21st Century: Issues of Inclusion and Reform*. Washington, DC: Gallaudet University Press.

Woodward, Stephanie. 2008. "Ronald Mace and His Impact on Universal Design." Center for Disability Rights, Inc. (Dec. 17), available at http://www.cdrnys.org.

Yatham, Lakshmi. 2010. *Bipolar Disorder*. New York: Wiley.

Zarb, Gerry. 1992. "On the Road to Damascus: First Steps Towards Changing the Relations of Research Production." *Disability, Handicap, and Society* 7: 125–138.

Zitzelsberger, Hilde. 2005. "(In)visibility: Accounts of Embodiment of Women with Physical Disabilities and Differences." *Disability & Society* 20: 389–403.

Index

About the Authors

Ronald J. Berger is professor of sociology at the University of Wisconsin-Whitewater. He has published more than 50 journal articles and book chapters, as well as 15 books, including *Introducing Disability Studies; Hoop Dreams on Wheels: Disability and the Competitive Wheelchair Athlete; Wheelchair Warrior: Gangs, Disability and Basketball* (with Melvin Juette); and *Storytelling Sociology: Narrative as Social Inquiry* (with Richard Quinney). Berger is also the recipient of the Wisconsin Sociological Association's William H. Sewell Outstanding Scholarship Award.

Jon A. Feucht earned his master's degree in special education at the University of Wisconsin-Whitewater and is currently a doctoral student in educational leadership and policy at East Tennessee State University. He is also the founding director of Authentic Voices of America, an innovative summer camp for adolescents and young adults learning to use augmentative communication devices. Feucht's publications include *Straight Talks*, a book of his speeches, and *The Tan Car*, a book of his poems, as well as articles in *Disability Studies Quarterly*, *Qualitative Inquiry*, and the *International Review of Qualitative Research*.

Jennifer Flad is assistant professor of sociology at the University of Wisconsin-Whitewater. Her previous publications have appeared in *Disability Studies Quarterly*, *Studies in Symbolic Interaction*, *Sociological Imagination*, and the *International Journal of Psychiatry in Medicine*. Flad is also the recipient of the Wisconsin Sociological Association's Hans O. Mauksch Outstanding Teaching Award.